The Camino Connection

Connecting with Life and Commemorating a Death While Walking on the Camino de Santiago

Lele Beutel

Lele Beutel loves to meet and chat with fans! Reach out to her at apedersen6@comcast.net.

Book Cover by Tatiana Vila

Print ISBN: 979-8-9902359-0-8
Ebook ISBN: 979-8-9902359-1-5

First edition 2024

Comments about The Camino Connection...

"As a pilgrim, I deeply appreciate the author's gift for transporting me into her journey. As a Christian, her narrative resonates as a testament to her role as a "secret angel for God." I've never met her son Phil, but she skillfully weaves a narrative that fosters a sense of love. The author depicts the transformative power of the Camino, showing how this sacred pilgrimage can cleanse the depths of one's soul and provide a path forward after such a heartbreaking loss."

—*Patrick DeVaney*, author of ***Two Million Steps: Band-aids, Cocktails, and Finding Peace Along Spain's Camino de Santiago***

"*The Camino Connection* is a testament to the enduring power of love. Despite the profound loss of her son in 2013, Lele's journey on the Camino de Santiago in 2023 shows the importance of her faith and the joy she receives as she treasures memories of her son. Lele's Camino story is not a selfish one, however, but reflects her genuine interest in her fellow humans and shows her loving dedication to friends new and old as she connects with others on her journey. This book is a heartfelt celebration of life, relationships, and faith."

—*Gordon J. Bernhardt*, author of ***Buen Camino: What a Hike through Spain Taught Me about Investing and Life***

"There are as many different Caminos as there are people who walk them. Lele's unique Camino is traveled as a 70-year-old woman who is grieving the loss of her adult son. Reading Lele's book about her Camino is like reading her diary. The detailed day-to-day accounts of her journey are punctuated with tidbits of information about the history of some of the places she passed through. Her connections with other pilgrims stands out as an important part of her experience."

—*Suzanne Blazier*, author of ***Prancing in the Pyrénées, Sloshing Through Galicia: My Way Along the Camino Francés***

"Lele's story is a moving account of her journey along the Camino de Santiago, the ancient pilgrim trail in northern Spain. For her, it was a journey of Healing—from the tragic loss of her son Phil—but it was also a journey of Connection.

"Not only does she vividly describe her walk—the things she saw, the places in which she stayed, the exotic foods she discovered—but she also frankly shares with the reader her emotions and experiences along the pilgrim trail. For those unable to undertake this journey, her story allows you to vicariously experience it from your own home. For those who might consider walking the Camino, her story will certainly whet your appetite and encourage you to consider walking the Camino yourself!"

—*Dr. Sanjiva Wijesinha*, author of ***Strangers on the Camino: A Father, a Son—and a Holy Trail***

"In *The Camino Connection*, Lele Beutel describes how faith guides her and a friend along several early sections of the Camino de Santiago, then she journeys mostly on her own from Sarria to Santiago de Compostela. The author walks for religious reasons and to honor her son's memory. She includes abundant historical references and animated details about her encounters with fellow pilgrims. Those who follow the Camino for religious significance will be drawn to her account."

—*Reginald Spittle,* author of **Camino Sunrise, Walking With My Shadows**

Dedicated to my son, Phil,
whose life brought light and hope,
even when others could see neither one.

Philip Hastings
1979-2013

And for those who are willing
to "go the distance"
so they can experience more of life...

Out in the Fields with God

The little cares that fretted me,
I lost them yesterday,
Among the fields, above the sea,
Among the winds at play;
Among the lowing of the herds,
The rustling of the trees;
Among the singing of the birds,
The humming of the bees.
The foolish fears of what may happen,
I cast them all away
Among the clover-scented grass,
Among the new-mown hay;
Among the rustling of the corn,
Where drowsy poppies nod,
Where ill thoughts die and good are born—
Out in the fields with God.

—Elizabeth Barrett Browning

Acknowledgements

Heartfelt thanks to the people who encouraged me in this project and took the time to give me helpful feedback. I appreciate the constructive input I received from *Bret Kolman, Jamie Kidd, Susan Edgar, and Suzanne and Charlie Barrett.* Other Camino book authors also contributed their time, effort, and thoughts regarding *The Camino Connection*. For these I am very thankful: *Suzanne Blazier, Reginald Spittle, Dr. Sanjiva Wajesinha, Patrick DeVaney,* and *Gordon J. Bernhardt.*

I also want to thank the very talented *Morris Jensen* for his wonderful artistic contribution to the book: the map. He spent many hours coming up with this enhancement for the book.

As an author, one is always grateful for any words of encouragement—these spurred me on to keep going. Thanks to all the people who contributed in this way, including my husband, Mike, who was my greatest cheerleader before, during, and after the Camino.

A map of the Camino Francés with a few of the stops along the way...

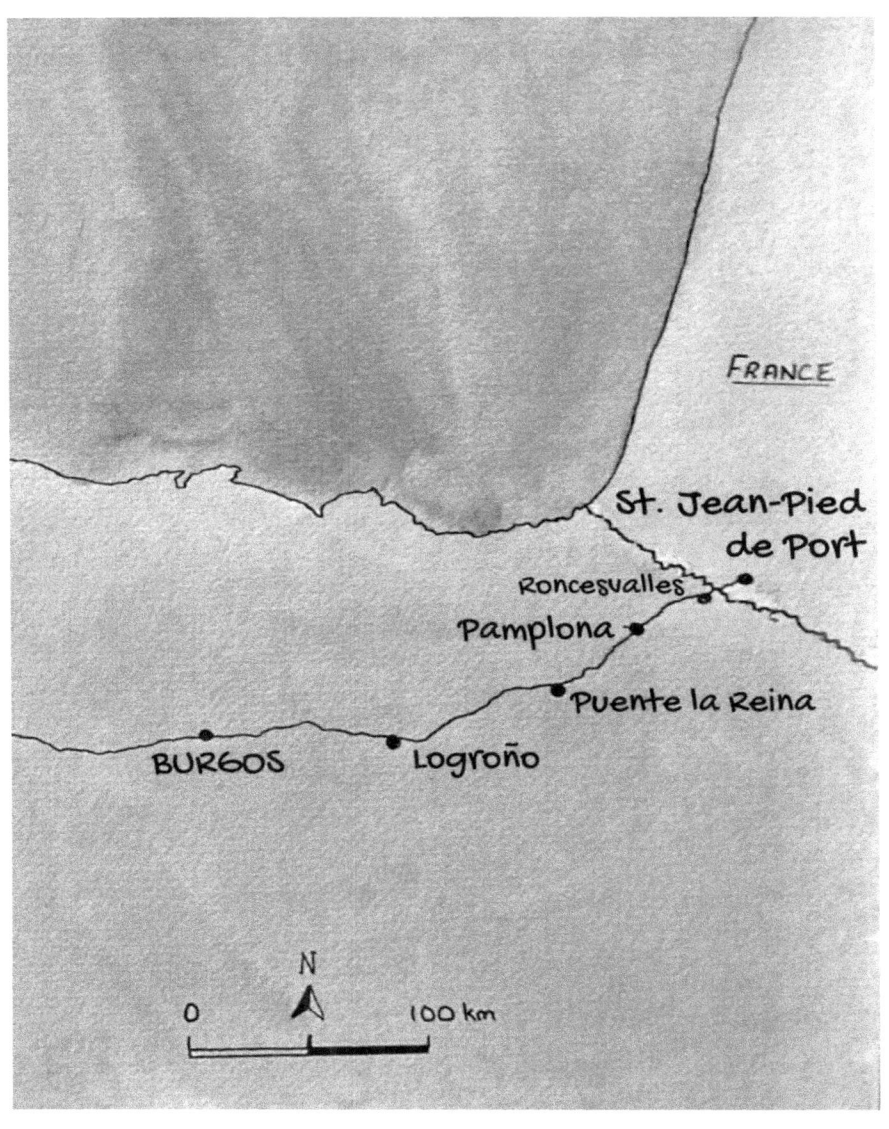

FRANCE

St. Jean-Pied
de Port

Roncesvalles

Pamplona

Puente la Reina

BURGOS   Logroño

N

0   100 km

Drawing by Morris Jensen

INTRODUCTION

"To feel the pull, the draw, the interior attraction, and to want to follow it, even if it has no name still, that is the 'pilgrim spirit.' The 'why' only becomes clear as time passes, only long after the walking is over."

—Kevin A. Codd in **Beyond Even the Stars**

*H*er eyes filled with tears as she blinked across at me. We sat at a rough hewn wood table in a restaurant in Orisson, the only stop between St. Jean Pied de Port and Roncevalles, France, on the first day of walking the Camino de Santiago.

"I can't do this," her voice shook. Hearing her words, my whole body tensed up in response, with a combination of anxiety, resistance, and empathy.

"It's too hard," she said. "I just don't think I can go any farther."

I knew Rachel was restraining herself and hiding what she could not explain to me—how much her hips and knees hurt. I could see this in the many times she had stopped and leaned over her hiking poles while she grimaced *and breathed heavily. And I had watched and waited for her so many times along the way....*

It had been an incredible, breath-taking, and grueling slog over the Pyrenees, all uphill from 594 feet to an elevation of 3,614 feet. Some of the climb was over asphalt roads, but much of it was over rock-pocketed dirt trails, where you had to make sure you stepped just the right way, so you didn't fall or trip or slide.

I braced myself now. How should I answer her? Could we continue this terribly difficult part of the journey? And, if we did, could we keep going over the next few days? Could I convince her and myself that it was possible? Was I willing to stop now or go back? Hadn't I warned her how difficult and challenging it would be?

"We can do this," I heard myself say. And I knew I was trying to convince both of us. I did not want to go back to St. Jean Pied de Port, where we'd started. I wanted to press on...if we could. I didn't want to be a quitter. We had to at least try! It had always been my nature to finish whatever I started.

"We can go slow if we need to." I said as I thought of all the possibilities and this one seemed the most reasonable. We just had to get to Roncevalles by nightfall. This was where our luggage would be waiting, along with the accommodations we'd booked ahead of time. And it was too late to change our reservations.

She gave me a very pained look. And my heart went out to her. But I was determined.

"For God's sake," I said to myself. "We've come this far! I don't want to go back!" But I also questioned if we could continue the trek. We'd only conquered five miles of the 15-mile walk for that day!

In 2010, I was inspired by a movie called *The Way,* about a father whose son dies on these same mountains, while walking the first day of the Camino de Santiago. To honor his son's passing, the father, Tom, played by Martin Sheen, decides to walk over the same trail. As I watched the movie, I began thinking about what it would be like to walk the Camino myself. Seeing how the father's life was transformed by the people he met and how he reflected on the memories of his son in a meaningful way, I was inspired and never forgot the feeling I had while watching the movie.

So, what was the "draw" of this unique journey for him, his son, and to others? I wondered back then, and, curious, I began to read more about the significance of this pilgrimage and why it means so much to so many people who walk it every year. The traditional Camino de Santiago, or Camino Francés, goes from St. Jean Pied de Port, France, to Santiago de Compostela, Spain, and is known as *The Way of St. James.* This is because many believe the apostle walked along this path centuries ago. Recently, I read a good explanation of the story surrounding St. James. In his book, *Walking with Sam*, Andrew McCarthy explains the background of the destination: "In the year 813 AD, in the far western reach of Spain, a hermit named Pelayo followed a ray of light that led him to a cave. There, he discovered the long-forgotten remains of the Apostle James.... Legend goes on to tell us that after Christ's crucifixion, resurrection, and ascension, James headed off to the Iberian Peninsula in order to preach the Word. But he...attracted just seven disciples for his troubles. Fortunately, the Virgin Mary appeared to James...[and] convinced him to return to Judea, where he was soon martyred by King Herod Agrippa's sword in the year 44.... Angels then carried his body—and decapitated head—and placed it in a stone boat. They guided it safely across the sea and back to Spain.... On arrival, a few of James's remaining disciples took the body and buried it in a nearby cave, where it remained undisturbed and forgotten for eight hundred years—until Pelayo came along.... The hermit/ shepherd notified the local priest of his discovery. The bishop authenticated the relics. King Alfonso II built a chapel, and the devout came running, or rather, walking. By the eleventh century, a thousand pilgrims a day were reaching Santiago, inspired by the plenary indulgences promising the complete remission of temporal punishment for successful completion of the pilgrimage. In short, a lot of time in purgatory could be spared by a good long walk."

Many myths surrounding the Camino have gone by the wayside, but a few traditions have remained. One of them has been, upon arrival at the Catedral de Santiago, to place one's hand into the base of the Tree of Jesse, or Christ's family tree, carved into the central column inside the main entrance of the cathedral by a Romanesque sculptor, Master Mateo, in 1188. Another is to touch one's head to the head of Master Mateo's statue inside the cathedral's portico to gain some of his genius. And another is to climb the steps behind the altar and embrace the statue of St. James, giving thanks for safe passage and offering prayers for those who helped you along the way. Sadly, these observances are no longer allowed due to erosion of the artwork. But the heart of the pilgrimage remains the same today: to lay down one's burdens at the feet of St. James in the cathedral, and, in essence, to place them at the feet of our savior, the Lord Jesus Christ.

The significance of the name *Santiago de Compostela*? *Compostela* comes from the Latin word, *campo*, which means "field," and *stella* meaning "star," to form the name that means "field of stars." Why? Because, when Pelayo (also referred to as the monk Pelagius) followed the ray of light that led him to St. James' bones, he beheld stars dancing over the field that is now called *Compostela*. *Santiago* comes from the Latin version of the name "James," or *Jacobus*, which evolved into *Iago* and was combined with *San* for "saint" to become *San-Iago* or *Santiago*.

Martin Sheen, after his role in *The Way*, was interviewed by a reporter from the National Catholic Register. He said, "Every pilgrimage is a journey to your own heart." Pilgrimage theologian Piotr Rozak is quoted as saying, "What a person discovers on the way to a holy place...is the experience of being guided by God."[1] Kevin A. Codd, in *To the Field of Stars*, says, "the walk to the Field of Stars, to Santiago de Compostela, is a journey that has the power to change lives forever."

The idea of walking the Camino was ignited again after my son, Phil, passed away in 2013 from lung cancer. I had grown to love daily walks around a lake near my house, which I'd started in 2004, after feeling God prompting me to take an hour every morning to "walk and pray," especially after Phil's first diagnosis of a tumor in one lung. It was because of these quiet times of contemplation that I was able to come to grips then and later with so many questions I had as to why my son suffered and died. I know many people blame God for the death and suffering of their loved ones. It was in my conversations with Him each day that I came to the realization that He never intended any of us to experience these terrible outcomes. And that He grieves as much as we do over the upsetting things that happen, which are often the result of our own or others' bad choices, apart from Him and over time. These heart-to-heart talks, along with daily searches through scriptures for answers, were extremely freeing for me.

But, in the days, weeks, months, and years after his death, I was still often overwhelmed by thoughts of regret, especially regarding the days before his passing. Often sounds or sights would trigger my mind to quickly zoom back to my last 10 days with him, when I went to stay with him, his wife, their two-year-old twin boys, and their newborn daughter. I slept in the only place available in the house: on the floor next to a crib in a tiny room on a deflating air mattress. Every day my back hurt more, and it grew harder each morning to get up. Often the twins would cry at night, and I tried to pry myself off the floor to get up and help. But their mother, who slept in the living room with the baby in a bassinette beside her, because

---

1. *ncregister.com, "'The Way' Returns to Theaters—Because Pilgrimage is Always a Good Idea"*

she couldn't sleep in the bedroom with Phil, whose breathing was very labored, would get to them before I could. Reflecting back, I know this was an excruciatingly painful time for her too.

Besides the physical challenges, I dealt with many mental and emotional ones too. I had watched the health of my physically robust son decline quickly over the course of a year, prompting me to increase the frequency of my visits between April and November of 2013. He lost a considerable amount of weight during this time, so that, on this last visit, he was just skin and bones, very frail, and mostly bed ridden.

One day, he asked me to take him to the bank to get the title to his beloved red truck. He knew he had to sell it. Portable oxygen tank in tow, he climbed beside me in my car, and we drove off to the bank. I walked in with him, and, when a manager asked him to go inside a vault with his key to get the title, I went outside to cry. It was so hard to watch him as he struggled to breathe through the tank on his back. And I thought about how much he loved his red truck but had obviously given up hope of ever driving it again. He knew the end was near. This broke my heart.

On the way home, he said, "Let's get some tacos!" And we pulled into a Burger King drive-through lane.

"Here?' I asked, eyebrows raised.

"Yes, they have the best tacos!" he informed me.

So, we bought enough tacos for ourselves and some to take home, and we enjoyed ours while sitting in the car. I was just happy he had an appetite. I will never forget this moment. Even as he had just resigned himself to selling his truck, he still enjoyed a moment with me...eating tacos!

Another time I will never forget during that last week together was when Phil asked me to sing the lyrics to his favorite songs while he and a neighbor, who came to spend time with him, strummed the tunes on their guitars. As they played "Face to Face," "I Come to the Garden Alone," and "Farther Along," I recorded them with my voice in the background singing the words to the songs, since Phil could no longer sing. I still have that recording on my phone.

But, later that week, tensions rose, along with relatives' reactions. One afternoon, my ex-husband, who lived in Denver and came to visit Phil often, grew angry with others who, he felt, were asking too much of Phil in his declining condition. Anger and accusations intensified, and the environment became very hostile and unforgiving. And any advice or suggestions I offered went unheeded and seemed to backfire, increasing the volatility. It got so bad that, one morning, I excused myself and drove the nine hours home from Denver to Kansas City in one day.

The night before I left, I had lain awake all night, after a heated family meeting led by Phil's minister-friend and mentor, Richard, who tried his best to run interference between family members' angry accusations. During one particularly hurtful moment, my son, who'd stood by my side for many years, joined in the attack against me for things I'd said and done. That was the last straw for me. That night, I felt like I was on the verge of a heart attack—my heart hurt so badly. I couldn't breathe. The verse that kept running through my mind all night long was Proverbs 4:23: *"Above everything else guard your heart, because from it flow the springs of life."* (*International Standard Version*) I believed God was telling me to protect my heart, and I knew I had to separate myself for a few days. Besides which a crown had fallen off one tooth, and I desperately needed some dental work done. And the clients in the office I'd birthed could not be indefinitely neglected. So, I rushed home, with the intention of returning within the next few days, at least in time to celebrate Thanksgiving with them. I felt like they needed some space, and so did I!

A few days later, Richard called. He was checking in on Phil every day, and I'd asked him to call me if he saw Phil's health declining rapidly and thought I should return right away.

"You need to come back now!" he said with urgency in his voice. Phil's health had slid so much that he was now in a hospice facility. So, my husband and I hopped in our car that afternoon and drove until midnight. When we got there, a kind nurse escorted us promptly into Phil's room, and we spent over an hour with him, watching old episodes of *Seinfeld*, his favorite TV show, feeding him orange sherbet, watching him laboriously breath through a tube in his nose, and holding his hand. I remember gazing down at his right hand and noticing the birthmark in the same place as one I had.

Around 1:30 am, the nurse suggested we leave to let him rest. Having company was stressful for him, she said. Hesitating, we followed her advice and went to a motel to try to sleep. My phone rang at 6:30 am, and I grabbed it. I was already up and preparing to return to Phil's side. It was the nurse.

"Phil passed away at 5:30 this morning," she said. My mind went numb. My heart raced. My body froze. I didn't want to believe it. We dressed and left as quickly as we could. In his room, we sat by his side for a long time, and I held his hand once again. But this time it was lifeless. I didn't care. I didn't want to leave his side. When we knew it was finally time, and we had to go, I burst out in tearful sobs as we walked down to hall.

"I'll never see him again!" I gushed and blurted out. "He's gone!"

When I told Phil the morning I left his house that I had to "regroup," he begged me to stay. I just couldn't, I said, and I stood firm. I insisted we all needed space. Over the years as I looked back at that horrible time, I often thought I should have stayed, in spite of the intense mental and physical pressures I felt. Often, when I take my dogs to the kennel for boarding, one or both of them will slink back in resistance at the front desk as if to say, "Don't leave us here, Mama! Please don't go!" and I think back on my son's pleas, and my heart freezes.

I realize now where the pressures I felt came from then and how I was in a fierce spiritual battle around the life of my son. Phil needed me, but I was sidetracked by others who distracted me from my reason for being there.

I wish I'd prayed more with him. And read more scripture together. And just sat by his side.

His wife told me after he died that he had held out to see me one last time. Then he let go.

Thinking about walking on the Camino, I often wondered if I, like Tom in *The Way*, could receive a healing release from the lingering, painful memories and regrets that continued to grip parts of my heart. If I did a pilgrimage like this, would it enable me to finally lay down this awful burden? I wondered. And the idea simmered in a secret place for almost 10 years!

Fast forward to June of 2022. While sitting at breakfast one morning during a company retreat, a colleague at my table named Rachel grabbed my attention.

"I would like to walk the Camino de Santiago," she said out of the blue.

"So would I," I quickly responded.

"Would you do it with me?" she asked, catching me by surprise.

Immediately hit with doubts, like, "I don't know her that well" and "My husband can't walk that far," I responded with "Yeah, but Mike can't do it."

A few weeks later, at dinner with a friend as we celebrated her husband's birthday, I mentioned another movie I'd watched recently, prompted by Rachel's idea of walking the Camino, called *I'll Push You*—a compelling documentary about two friends who decide to experience the Camino together, one in a wheelchair due to a crippling disease and the other willing to push his friend. The movie reconstructs how the two, with the help of others, crossed all 500 miles from St. Jean Pied de Port to Santiago de Compostela, often experiencing extreme hardships and rough conditions.

"You've always wanted to do the Camino," my friend said. "I can do it with you!"

"Really?" I looked over at her, completely taken off guard.

"Yes," she responded. "Go ahead and make plans, and I'll join you!"

So, feeling spurred on, I began to investigate the ways it could be done. My criteria included working with an outfit that could book good places for us to stay along the way. I wanted to avoid albergues.

Albergues are popular with travelers who want to "rough it" pilgrim-style and don't want to plan ahead as far as the distance they will walk each day. But, like hostels, they often mean staying in large rooms filled with bunkbeds for 20-40 or more people who may snore, help themselves to your gear, and carry bedbugs. Not for us, I decided. And, not at my age. I would turn 70 before the trip.

I also wanted someone to arrange the transport of our luggage each day from one hotel to the next so that all we'd have to carry was a daypack. After some research, I decided that Mac's Adventures out of Glasgow, Scotland, offered what we needed.

As I began planning, I decided to reach out to Rachel and let her know about our plans. I didn't want her to find out later and be disappointed that my friend and I had made the trek without letting her know. When I called her, she said quickly, "Count me in!" So, I arranged a time we could all meet and discuss the possibilities.

We met for lunch and, over salads at a restaurant, I shared what I'd discovered. Walking the entire Camino takes about 35 days. Since we were all limited in how much time we could take to do the trek (we'd agreed on no more than two weeks), we agreed on a "best of" trip where we spent one week walking from St. Jean Pied de Port to Logroño, Spain, with a transport that would take us from Logroño to Sarria, Spain. Then we'd spend the second week walking from Sarria to Santiago, about 62 miles, which was the minimum distance to be able to receive a coveted certificate in Santiago for traversing the Camino. We would shoot for the second and third weeks in May 2023. So began our plans....

Until I got a call from my friend. She confessed that she'd tried climbing uphill for a few hours and was experiencing a great deal of hip pain.

"I don't think I can do it," she confessed. "I'm going to opt out."

She'd also realized that she had some conflicts with the time we were talking about going. I called Rachel to let her know.

"I'm still in!" Rachel responded.

"Ok. So am I," I committed. I didn't want to be the one to disrupt what we'd started.

And so, the plans continued for what would turn out to be a life-changing, heart-healing journey of a lifetime.

STEP ONE

PREPARE US FOR
"GOD KNOWS WHAT!"

"When we are getting ready to embark on a faith journey, God does not leave us empty-handed."

—Brian Simmons in **Courage to Conquer**

After the initial get-together, Rachel and I began discussing travel plans. In September 2022, we decided that May 5-24 worked best with our schedules, so we booked our trip with Mac's. In January 2023, we scheduled a call with a travel agent, who helped us book flights through Paris to Biarritz, France, and back through Vigo and Madrid, Spain. So far so good.

We compared notes on gear. What backpacks and luggage might work best? Should we take our hiking poles? What pants, jackets, shirts, socks, hats, and shoes would be suitable? What about "hiking wool" for blisters? What's the best kind of water bottle to bring? How much stuff should we take? We knew we wanted to carry on what we were taking, so we had to limit the size of our suitcases and backpacks. We sifted through them and gradually eliminated what wasn't absolutely necessary. I wanted to take two pairs of good hiking shoes, in case one got wet or worn out. This ended up being a good idea. I'd wear one pair, but the other packed pair took up some room in my suitcase. So, I had to work around them. We walked together some Saturdays, finding a trail with some uphill hiking.

"Do you feel like you're ready?" I asked on one walk through a wooded area as we tried out our hiking poles. I was concerned about our huffing and puffing as we made our way up a hill.

"Yes, and you?" she responded.

"As ready as I can be," I asserted.

But I continued to have concerns about our preparedness, especially after reading more about the first day of the Camino. The route that we wanted to take ascended up and over the Pyrenees for a distance of 15 miles, and I knew for sure that would be a grueling day. I thought about my age. And I wondered how my sometimes-aching hips would fare as I made my way up so many miles all at once. Rachel, at 58, had knee issues and had had cortisone treatments, but her doctor encouraged her to walk. I wondered if this first day challenge might prove to be the greatest physical, mental, and spiritual battle that I would need to overcome!

Then, my husband brought up another concern.

"What if you have to use the bathroom and there aren't any available?" He posed a question I'd never verbalized. I'd never read of anyone having a problem with this while walking the trail, but maybe their needs weren't as urgent as mine sometimes were. My husband knew me well.

"Hmmm..." I wondered without answering him because I didn't know. Another thing God would have to help me with, I thought, in addition to all the other things. Sometimes I asked myself why I was going on this trip. Was it to satisfy Rachel's desire to make the trek? Or was it for my own reasons, like making a life transition into retirement or finally releasing the regret-burden for my son? I searched my heart on the matter and decided that, although her initial proposal had set the idea into motion, I also had wanted to do this for many years, and now might be the only opportunity I had to check this off my bucket list. I would do it for myself as well, I concluded. And, while I was at it, I'd make it very meaningful. But how? I pondered this question before, during, and after the journey. It wasn't until we'd completed the walk that I really understood what it was all about. And it all became crystal-clear when I reflected back on the experience. Now, I considered, would it be more of a spiritual, mental, or physical journey for me? Or could it somehow be all three?

As my questions grew, we proceeded with our plans. In April 2023, nine days before we left, I came across a miraculous find. As I walked one of our dogs around the lake near my house, I happened to look down beside the sidewalk when we stopped at a corner and spotted something half-buried in the dirt. It was colorful and caught my eye, so I bent down to pick it up. It turned out to be a shell painted blue with yellow designs on it, the same colors as the shell-signs that mark the trails for the Camino. Even the designs were like those on the signs I'd later see in Spain. I turned the shell over and saw that someone had written a verse: Philippians 4:13. I knew it by heart: *"I can do all things through Christ who strengthens me."* When I looked the verse up in *The Amplified Bible,* it grew into even greater significance. There, it reads: *"I have strength for all things in Christ Who empowers me [I am ready for anything and equal to anything through Him Who infuses inner strength into me; I am self-sufficient in Christ's sufficiency.]"* Wow! I wondered what it meant for me, and I took it as a message that only God could send in this way. It seemed to be the confirmation of a promise that I would have the strength and endurance to walk the Camino. And, that I would discover the reasons I needed to do it. He would disclose these to me along the way.

The shell I found while walking

Six days before leaving, I passed the shell around a friend's living room so the people in our church life group could see it. After oohing and aahing over its significance, they all prayed for my journey and the weather, which caused me some concern when I looked at my weather app and saw that it might be very rainy and cold in parts of Spain.

"Thanks for hearing our prayers, Lord!" I wrote in my journal. "Give us a very successful and blessed journey. Thanks for being with us!"

I made sure to tuck this meaningful shell into an inside pocket of my backpack. I wanted to carry it along as a reminder of God's promises to me. I thought of leaving it behind in a special place along the trail to commemorate my son, but I couldn't bring myself to part with it. So, I found a simple scallop shell, wrote a message on it, and tucked it deep down in my backpack. I would leave this one at the right place along the way...for my son.

Five days before we left, I wrote down what I felt God was speaking into my spirit: "Don't worry so much about the weather on your trip. Do you believe I will take care of you? Of course, I will! I'll be in every step you take! And place you where I want you. So don't feel anxious or concerned. Know that I am with you! Know that every detail is in My hands, including your health and well-being. I will give you strength. Because you are so precious to Me! I love you!"

"Look for the signposts along the way to direct you as to where to go and what to avoid," a friend said when I told her about the trip. "It will be clear. God will open your spiritual eyes to what you need to see. He will also lead you to people who are looking for answers that you can give them. You will see miracles. Watch and see!"

Three days before we left, I reflected on my transition into retirement and how I needed to smoothly move this year from a busy work-a-day schedule to one that was completely self-determined. My clients kept warning me that I would be bored after a while, and I did not want that to happen. I wanted to spend my remaining years wisely and productively and feel like my life still mattered. As I opened up one of my devotionals, I was amazed to find a quote that summarized what I was feeling. In Brian Simmons' book, *Courage to Conquer*, he wrote: "Is there a transition that you are making? Do you want to move on mindfully, not just rushing ahead to the next thing? Let reflection move you toward gratitude. Write down the best moments, along with the worst, and their corresponding lessons. Think through what you want to take with you and what you want to leave behind. Let the Spirit of God lead you to the treasure of his wisdom, both on display and hidden in your story, and share it with those it will encourage."

I wrote beside it, "This is what I want to accomplish while walking on the Camino de Santiago!" It was clear that this would be a significant part of the mental and spiritual goals I wanted to achieve. I also reflected back on the desire I'd held for over 10 years, and I wondered if, in this journey, I might experience what I would consider the miraculous. Could I actually see my way to a meaningful and happy retirement by leaving behind the lingering regrets? Could I finally feel free to move ahead, holding onto only the good recollections from work and life, into a new and joyful season?

That evening, I went to a prayer night at our church. People who needed healing were asked to come up front. As I considered whether or not to go forward for prayer, my mind went back to my son and how we had hoped and prayed that he would be healed.

In 2001, doctors discovered a benign tumor in his lower left lung lobe. He'd been coughing uncontrollably, and they decided it needed to be removed. Five years later, he began coughing again, this time spewing blood. Another tumor was discovered, this time in the upper left lobe. And, this time, it was malignant. They decided to try chemotherapy, and, miraculously, the treatments came at little cost to him since he worked part-time delivering pizza and qualified for a medical program available to the "indigent." We believed God had worked this out for him and prayed for a cure. After months of debilitating infusions, the doctors determined that they were not shrinking the tumor, which had grown larger. In 2007, they removed the upper left lobe, which had been taken over by a large, obstructive tumor. If they didn't, the doctors said, eventually his trachea would be completely blocked by the growth.

He recovered from the second surgery, and our hope was that this might be the end of the cancer. But that changed in December 2008. I remember where I was when I got the news. I was placing cards around tables in a country club dining room, preparing for a Christmas dinner with a speaker for some of my clients for whom I served as their financial advisor. My cell phone rang; it was Phil. He always sounded upbeat, no matter what, but I could detect some stress in his voice.

"Mom, they found tumors in my right lungs." My heart froze as I tried to accept this information and what it meant. I just didn't know what to say.

"I am so sorry, Phil." I said numbly as I continued to set out cards.

That year, he met a woman and, even after he shared the details of his situation, she agreed to marry him. In February 2009, they were married. And Phil was ecstatic. He had always wanted a family and children. This was his dream. I remember writing in my journal, shortly after the wedding, that God had told me they'd have a boy. A year later, I was sitting in the Walmart parking lot when he called me.

"Mom, you were wrong!"

"Well, I've been wrong before!"

"Yea, this time you were really wrong. We're not having a boy. We're having *two* boys!" He laughed. I did too.

He and his wife had twin boys in March 2011.

But the tiny tumors on the right side continued to grow. During Thanksgiving of 2011, we took him to the emergency room when he struggled to breathe. It was after he'd been singing and playing the guitar. The doctors pointed out that the tumors were collecting along his lung lining and causing him pain. After that, he sought out advice from other doctors, but he was not eligible for the programs they offered. By early 2013, his breathing became more labored, and he was put on an oxygen machine. With each week, he grew thinner and weaker as he labored more and more for each breath. Our hearts broke to see this vigorous, light-hearted, faith-steady, joy-filled young man declining so quickly.

I remember one day when I was visiting him in Denver, and I drove to do an errand for him. I saw a healthy young man jogging down the street next to me. It was like he was running in slow motion as I watched him.

"Why can't that be Phil?" I cried. My heart ached.

Despite his failing health, Phil was always an example of hope. He witnessed his faith to the doctors and nurses, who grew to love him.

"He is the most positive person we've ever encountered," one doctor said of him.

Three weeks before he died, his daughter was born, and he was able to hold her. God had promised him that.

"I saw a very bright light," he told me as I sat on the bed beside him two weeks before he died. "It appeared to me in the hospital when she was born.

The words it gave me were, 'It's not the body that's most important. It's the spirit inside you that will live on.'"

Since his death in November 2013, I think often of these words spoken to him, and how his spirit does live on, and I look forward to seeing him again someday. This is the hope that keeps me going. It's the circumstances and questions surrounding his death that still burden me at times, and these are the weights that I must finally lay down.

I stepped forward for prayer that night at the church, and I could feel my hips aching and a sciatic nerve pinching and shooting pain down one leg. I stood by the stage with hundreds of others, singing songs and lifting my hands up, trying to ignore the pain. I could sense God's presence and hoped others could too. As the songs went on, I whispered a prayer.

"Lord, if you want me to keep standing here, You're going to have to heal my hurting hips and nerve! And, if You want me to sit on a plane for hours and walk miles up and down hills on trails in a foreign land, would You please get rid of this pain!"

As I stood there with my hands lifted up, persistently asking, He suddenly released me from the pain.

"Another miracle," I thought, "and more confirmation from Him!"

The day before we left, I wrote in my journal: "Wow! We leave tomorrow for France. Lord, be in each and every step, and reassure me of Your presence! I need Your helping hand to accomplish what's needed and bodily strength to do it! Give me grace on the planes and on the walk to be pain-free. Let everything go smoothly on this trip, Lord! I leave it all in Your hands. Thanks. I love You!"

My heart felt a little lighter, but I still had that unsettled, anxious feeling of not knowing what to expect. I knew this journey would be a life-changing one, but would it be disruptive in a good way, or would it be something I'd have to struggle to move past later, like my son's death?

STEP TWO

A PRECARIOUS PASSAGE TO ST. JEAN PIED DE PORT

"Traveling is a brutality. It forces you to trust strangers and to lose sight of all the familiar comforts of home and friends. You are constantly off balance. Nothing is yours except the essential things. Air, sleep, dream, the sea, the sky—all things tending towards the eternal or what we imagine of it."

—*Cesare Pavese*

"We leave today for France," I wrote in my journal the morning of May 5th. "And my heart feels a little anxious about it all. Thanks for all the reassurances, Lord! Thanks for giving me needed peace and being with us all along the way, and giving us signs, wonders, and assurances of Your presence. We need You in this! And strength, both physical and mental, to walk this journey. Bless what we do, what we say, and remind us that You are there! Teach us along the way too. Show us what You want for us. Thanks!"

I also recorded an odd dream I'd had the night before of leaving my phone somewhere and finding it with all my credit cards inside the case stolen. "Protect all that we have," I wrote. "Thanks, Lord! And open our eyes to what we need to see!"

The time came for our departure. My apprehensions lingered, but I tried to focus on the things God had shown and done for me so I could move ahead. I sighed as my husband dropped us off at the airport. We gathered our backpacks and suitcases and turned to watch him drive away after the goodbye hugs. Were we crazy? I wondered. Well, there was no turning back now. We were on our way! We grabbed some coffee and breakfast sandwiches on the way to the gate. As we waited to board the first flight from Kansas City to Atlanta, we heard our names being called out over the loudspeaker. We'd pulled up our passes on our phones, so we hadn't checked in at the ticket counter and had gone right through security, but they wanted to check us in here at the gate.

"You must always check in for an international flight," the agent said sharply.

On the second flight from Atlanta to Paris, I sat next to a couple from Yorkshire, England. This was my first taste of what God had in store for me. At first glance, the wife, a very cute, middle-aged blonde, with hair pulled back, seemed stuck up and shallow. But I felt prompted to start a conversation with her anyway and quickly discovered how very wrong my impression of her was. I asked about her background, and she revealed that she was a very savvy businesswoman who had single-handedly started a nonprofit agency in Britain to help many elderly people throughout the country. I was awed by what she'd done and realized once again how foolish it is to judge people by their appearance.

The Paris airport was challenging to maneuver, but we found our way to a shuttle that went to an outlying terminal where we boarded a regional flight to Biarritz. As we sat in a café in the Biarritz Airport, I shared some of my hopes with Rachel, then I asked what she wanted to see happen on this trip. She shared two things: she wanted to discover more about how to make daily time for prayer and meditation, and she wanted to lose weight. I thought about how I could encourage her with the first one. But, keeping weight off was an ongoing challenge for me, and I had come to terms with my current status. I was within the range for my age and height, so I'd decided that, if I lost weight, I'd be happy, but, if I didn't, I'd be ok with that too. So, I might not be of much help with this goal.

After our coffee break, we tried to figure out how to board a bus to Bayonne, where we could catch a train to St. Jean Pied de Port. No one spoke enough English in the airport to help us, and we attempted, without much success, to decipher charts on a wall and figure out which bus to take. I was learning not to be shy about asking for help, so I walked up to a young man with a backpack who was standing next to a chart that described the bus routes in French. As it turned out, he spoke some English, so I told him we were on our way to walk the Camino and asked if he knew which bus to take to Bayonne. He directed us to the right one, and we sighed with relief as we stepped through the open door and climbed the steps. But, once on the bus, we found it impossible to communicate with the driver that we needed to get off at the Bayonne train station. He shook his head indicating that he didn't understand a word we were saying. As we kept repeating our request with words and gestures, a young woman jumped up from her seat on the bus and came forward to translate for us. Finally, he understood and nodded. She was a Godsend at that moment, and we were thankful for her willingness to intervene. We sat down near the bus driver so we could see when he indicated for us to get off.

We drove for miles, and I saw signs for Bayonne with no nod or motion from the driver. After a while I grew concerned until he finally pointed toward a stop. I thanked him when the bus came to a screeching halt, and we jumped off. As the bus pulled away, we looked around the street where we stood, with our backpacks and luggage in tow, but could see no sign of a train station.

"What do we do now?" Rachel grew concerned.

"I'll ask someone where it is," I said, looking around.

"Can we trust anyone to understand us and give us good directions?" she asked.

"We have no choice," I said. "We'll have to depend on someone."

I noticed a sign on the corner with the word "Gare" on it, and I remembered from my high school French classes that it meant "train station." I turned to a man who was walking past us and asked, "Gare? Train station?" He quickly pointed up a street and indicated it was around the corner. I thanked God again for His help when it was totally unexpected through a random stranger.

Off we went, lugging our backpacks and thumping our luggage behind us over the cobbled streets. Sure enough, across this street, up and around a corner, stood a large train terminal. We walked inside and looked for a window to get our tickets. No one was behind the glass at what seemed to be the obvious place. Just then, we saw a woman approaching us hurriedly from the front of the station, loudly spattering unintelligible French.

"St. Jean Pied de Port?" I asked, trying to communicate what we needed. Many boisterous words and arm motions later, we were able to secure our tickets and decipher the destinations flashing on a board above us that the train to St. Jean Pied de Port would arrive in two hours. We wouldn't know until right before departure time what track it was on. Good luck!

We slumped into very hard wooden chairs along one wall of the uninviting, dirty terminal and found plugs to charge our dwindling phones. I almost fell asleep as we waited but could never get comfortable enough in the classroom-style seats. The time for our train came, and we pulled our luggage toward the platform. The arm-waving lady yelled toward us, and we headed for the steps that led under the tracks along with dozens of others, who rushed to get to the other side of the terminal to board the waiting trains. Under the platform, I identified a sign on the wall that pointed to the track for St. Jean Pied de Port, and I headed up the steps. Rachel followed. We asked a girl beside one train car if it was the one going to St. Jean, just to make sure we were on the right train. "Yes," she said, and we hopped on. The car was very crowded, and we sat on one side with our backs to the windows. A uniformed lady popped her head in and motioned for us to follow her to another less-crowded car. We did and found seats along the side right inside the door next to a young woman. We parked our luggage and backpacks on the other side of the train.

The train jolted forward, and we were on our way! When it stopped for a moment, I got up to get something out of my backpack. Just then the train lurched forward, and I fell backward with my lower back hitting the metal armrest on my chair. I staggered back into my seat. When I felt a sharp, shooting pain in my back, I prayed, "Lord, this will NOT stop me! Thanks for healing!" My back was sore and bruised for a while, but it never got in the way of my walking. I was very thankful for this.

The young woman sitting next to me on the train asked if we were walking on the Camino.

"Yes, and you?" I asked.

She was. She turned out to be 31 and from New Zealand. She was traveling alone to walk the trail, but then she was going on to other places in Europe as part of a sabbatical between jobs. She had just separated from a boyfriend, and this trip would be a needed respite from life as usual where she could regroup and discover what she needed to do going forward and in what direction she wanted her life to go. I thought of my own life and the reasons I'd decided to walk.

"Aren't we all looking to find our way?" I thought. "Aren't we all making some sort of transition in life and wondering if we are going down the right path?"

I have often reflected on these thoughts and asked God, "What did You want for me when I was born? How do You see me now? Would You help me with my choices today?" And sometimes I think it takes your whole life to discover these things and figure things out. And my prayer often is: "Just lead me and let me know if I am going the best way today!"

I was amazed that the girl from New Zealand had traveled so far by herself. Silently, I prayed for her trip and that she would find peace and direction. As I did, I thought of my son, who was 34 when he died, and, at one time, had wanted to travel to places like this and be on trains to destinations where he could backpack and walk and talk with God and other people. Like me, he wanted to discover more about his own life and who he was and where he was meant to be. Sadly, he never had time to do these things. And that was one of my heart-burdens for him.

In St. Jean Pied de Port, we stepped off the train along with many others. I turned as I deboarded to see more than a few individuals, like hamsters escaping from a cage-door left open, lunging from the train-car doors. Most of them hurried past a building with the name of the town on the side, but a few stopped for pictures under the sign. We were no exception. At a tiny restroom beside the building, I met two middle-aged women from Quebec. Their goals were like mine: discover how to successfully transition to a next step.

Arrived at St. Jean Pied de Port!

St. Jean Pied de Port, literally "Saint John at the Foot of the Pass," stands at the base of the Roncevaux (Roncevalles in Spanish) Pass across the Pyrenees. A town of only 1,510 as of 2020, it is the old capital of the traditional Basque province of lower Navarre, a geographically diverse region in northern Spain, and a starting point for the French Way, or Camino Francés, which is the most popular option for traveling the Camino de Santiago. The routes from Paris meet at St. Jean Pied de Port, and it is the pilgrims' last stop before climbing the mountains into Spain.

Rachel used her Maps app to find our hotel, just up the street, around a corner, past some restaurants, then up a hill and through an archway called the Porte de France. We struggled to find the entrance but located a door up some steps and approached the desk for Hotel Restaurante Ramuntcho. It was conveniently located near the town's main thoroughfare. Aged and quaint, our single rooms were small but comfortable with a twin bed, chair, wardrobe, and bathroom with tub and shower. My large window had a beautiful view of a courtyard full of flowers and many white-plastered buildings with red-tiled rooftops beyond. I immediately pushed aside the red shutters so that they folded into both sides of the window. Then I breathed in the fresh air. I loved how so many of the smaller, local inns in France and Spain have these shuttered windows that open up so guests can look out and experience the beauty outside. Gazing down at the courtyard, I watched as an older man tended to the plants.

The Porte de France | Outside my hotel window

After settling into our rooms, we met downstairs to venture out and find a place to dine. It was 4:30 pm and we hadn't eaten all day. We went back to a place we'd seen on our way to the hotel, where people sat outside around tables in a courtyard. It looked inviting. When we walked toward a table, we asked a woman carrying a tray if they were serving food. She shook her head. It was too early. We quickly discovered that most restaurants in France and Spain don't serve dinner until at least 7 or 8 o'clock at night.

We walked up the street and approached a waiter standing outside another café.

"Food?" I asked.

He nodded, and I grew excited.

"Basque burger!" he said enthusiastically.

"Great!" we both responded and quickly found seats at a table in front of the restaurant. He brought us the juiciest, most delicious hamburgers we'd ever experienced, along with thick, crunchy French fries. We toasted to our success so far with glasses full of Basque beer. We had arrived and we were in heaven!

After eating, we wandered farther down the main street, Rue de la Citadelle, that ran alongside our hotel to see an archway that led through the Notre-Dame Gate. Rachel recognized it from the movie, *The Way*. Past it, we found a bridge with wonderful views of the historical, white-plastered buildings with red shutters and tiled roofs that lined the River Nive. Back up the cobbled street toward our hotel, we found many quaint storefronts with decorated windows filled with pottery, specialty foods, jewelry, and Camino memorabilia. But we were exhausted, and our beds were calling to us.

Back in my room, I texted my husband. When we left, I was concerned about one of our dogs—a "shweenie," a Dachshund and Shih Tzu mix. He hadn't been eating and he was chewing on his paws. I wanted to know how he was.

"He's doing great," my husband texted back. "He's eaten, and I took him to the vet for an allergy shot."

I sighed with relief. Another thing I didn't have to worry about.

"Lord, thanks for taking care of Barney," I wrote in my journal that evening. "And for getting us here safely. And for a waiter willing to serve us some food!"

And I wondered again what we would discover at the Pilgrim's Office the next day and what they'd tell us about trekking over the Pyrenees on day one of our journey. I was concerned about the weather, and, before we left, I'd gritted my teeth when I read Mac's description of this more difficult way: "The toughest section…with a steep climb to Roncevalles…. Passes across the Pyrenees on a route called Ruta Imperial (Imperial Route). [We also heard it called the Napoleon Route.] You will be rewarded with wonderful panoramic mountain view and a great sense of achievement. An alternate route is available along the valley for those who prefer a gentler option."

Would they tell us if they thought it might be too challenging for us? Would they consider the weather predictions? Would my hips be able to manage the climb? And, what about Rachel's knees? Would someone at the office be honest enough to look at us and tell us if they thought we should take the easier route to Roncevalles? My mind whirred with questions and concerns.

STEP THREE

EXPLORING AND EATING IN ST. JEAN

"People walk the Camino for many reasons—but there are some common themes. Walking the Camino provides an opportunity of taking time off the mundane activities of a householder and being granted the space to think, to remember, to get to know oneself—and to reflect on the memory of loved ones."

—Sanjiva Wijesinha in **Strangers on the Camino**

It was May 8th. Monday. "I woke up a few times last night but was fully awake at 5:44 am," I wrote in my journal that night. "Got up. Washed my face, drank four small cups of water, dressed, read. Rachel texted at 7:20 to meet downstairs in 10 minutes. We went down to a wonderful, typically European breakfast: hard rolls, butter, all kinds of jam, dried fruit, coffee, juice, fruit cups, yoghurt, thin sliced ham, and cheese. All good!"

At 9 o'clock we set off for the Pilgrim's Office, just up the street from our hotel, at 39 Rue de la Citadelle. We passed a shop with promising hiking poles in the window. We decided to go back after getting our Camino passports. We'd left our poles at home, since we were required to check them at the airport, and we wanted to carry on all our luggage to avoid the problem of lost bags along the way.

At the Pilgrim's Office, we pulled open a large double door and stepped into a spacious room where several people sat on the other side of a long table talking with many pilgrims, often in couples, who sat across from them. I could hear different languages spoken on both sides of the counter. On the opposite side of the room from the table sat a few chairs and poles and backpacks propped against a wall. At the far side of the room was a shelf full of white scallop shells attached to red strings. Pilgrims were welcome to take and hang these on their knapsacks to show that they were walking on the Camino.

We stood next to a man from Portland, Oregon, as we waited for an available English-speaking attendant. He told us that he was getting ready to walk the entire Camino and had done this many times before. I guessed he was in his 60s. Soon, a short, blond woman, also in her 60s, motioned to us from behind the counter, and we took our seats in front of her. We squeezed between couples on either side of us. The perky attendant helped us fill out our Camino passports. Also called credentials, these are four-by-six-inch booklets with many accordion-style, folding pages where albergues, hotels, cafés, and shops along the Camino can place their official stamps as proof of your journey. She made sure we put our names and other pertinent info in the right places on the first page, then, after stamping them to show we'd officially checked in at the St. Jean Pilgrim Office, she gave us a cursory overview of walking the Napoleon Route over the Pyrenees. She described a few details of the route and made some bold marks on a map. I missed part of her explanations when I turned to see the young woman who sat beside us on the train standing behind me. I waved to her enthusiastically.

Turning back to the blond attendant, I asked what she thought of the weather predictions, which called for rain, and if she thought it safe to take the mountain route. She poopooed my question and acted like it was of no concern at all. Then she tried to humor us by hinting that, since we must be wealthy Americans, we should leave her a big tip. Later that day, we saw her at a store nearby shopping for jewelry.

After securing our passports and maps, we went back to the shop where we'd seen the hiking poles. When we stepped into Boutique du Pèlerin, the Camino Shop, we were greeted by a friendly, attractive, middle-aged woman, who hailed from Canada and had moved here to marry the shop owner. She turned out to be an expert in fitting people with the right hiking poles and explaining the best way to use them. We were thankful for her expertise. She showed us several options, and we chose poles decorated with scenes from the Camino trail, so "we'd never forget where we got them." I also found a baseball hat decorated with Camino insignia, a lightweight shirt, and a hooded fleece pullover, which I was very thankful for later, when the mornings were cooler than I expected.

One other item I purchased, that grew in its significance as I learned more about it, was a special Camino shell on a long red string. The one I chose, unlike the ones at the Pilgrim's Office, had an unusual red cross painted on it. I wanted this one because I'd seen others with it swinging from their backpacks, and I felt like it accurately represented how I perceived this journey—as mostly a spiritual one.

I found out later that the scallop, with its many grooves that move to a central point at the top, represents all the different Camino trails that a pilgrim can walk, including the traditional one we chose from St. Jean Pied de Port to Santiago de Compostela. I read that the longest route stretches from Paris to Santiago, but I heard of people coming from even farther away and then walking back home! The scallop was also used by pilgrims at one time to scoop up water from streams and fountains to drink along the way.

A Camino shell

I looked into the history of the symbolic red cross and found out that it's called the *Cross of St. James* and shows up throughout Spain on coats of arms and special *Tarta de Santiago*, or Spanish almond cakes that honor Camino pilgrims. Most think its cross and sword design symbolizes the defense of faith and the use of weapons to defend it. Some say the sword also represents the one used by King Herod Agrippa to decapitate St. James.

Either way, its striking red color stands for the blood shed by the martyred apostle. The body of the cross—a sword that points down with fleur-de-lis on the top and sides of the hilt— originated with the Order of the Knights of Santiago in 1170. An offshoot of the Knights Templar, the order's objectives were to protect pilgrims along the Camino and to provide them with shelter, food, and spiritual guidance. As it turns out, a big part of Spain's history involves efforts by Christian leaders, like Charlemagne, to push back the Muslims, or Moors, while defending the Christian troops. In 1175, Pope Alexander III approved the order's rules, which included the adoption of the red cross as a symbol to identify the order. According to legend, in 844, St. James appeared on a white horse carrying a white flag with a red cross and helped the Christians prevail against the Moors in the Battle of Clavijo. This legend led to another of St. James' names, *Matamoros*, or "killer of Moors." Others think the cross originated with the Crusades, when knights carried crosses with sharp ends so they could plant them in the ground.

For me, the cross and its color symbolized Christ and what He gave—His life's blood so we could live life the way God meant it to be lived with Him at the center—and the sword stood for God's Word, which is our "sword of the spirit."

I left the shop with a bag of clothes, poles, and the special scallop in hand. It was still early, so we found a welcoming café, where we ordered cappuccinos, or café crème as they are called in France, from a cheerful young man, who reminded me of my son. Then we sat in a lovely courtyard surrounded by white-plastered walls, with the underlying stones peeking through in spots and a gaping, red-shuttered window peering down above us. We relished the charm of the place as we sipped from steaming cups of delicious coffee.

Then we walked back up Rue de la Citadelle, past the Pilgrim's Office and many quaint, white-plastered houses with green shutters and large pots of pink, yellow, orange, and red flowers lined up in front. At the end of the street, we discovered a rough stone-laid path with a series of stone steps that led up to an ancient citadel at the top of a hill. A massive arch with open gates greeted us at the summit and invited us toward a timeworn structure.

La Citadelle de St. Jean Pied de Port was built in 1628 as a fort, then rebuilt in 1680. Now it serves as a secondary school and is closed to the public. Though we couldn't peek inside the massive doors, our efforts were rewarded by a spectacular view of the town and the surrounding hills. I sighed with delight as I looked down at hundreds of white-washed buildings topped with red-tile roofs surrounded by lush, green hills that rose up to the cloudy sky. As the hills ascended to the clouds, lighter-green verdure became darker-green wooded areas that embraced the mountains' many meadows.

An informative map on a platform at the very top of the hill showed us what towns lay beyond this one. We realized how close Roncevalles, our next stop, really was.

"You know, it's only 17 miles away!" Rachel reminded me. "But we have to climb a mountain to get to it!"

I thought about that and how quickly we could get there if we were driving.

We descended the hill and decided to go to the other end of town. Down Rue de la Citadelle, past L'Eglise Notre Dame du Bout du Pont, a beautiful and historic old church, through the Notre Dame Gate, then over the River Nive bridge, we appreciated again the charming view along the river.

Through the Notre-Dame Gate

We approached a path that led to a more rustic bridge and a sign with an arrow pointing to the Camino trail.

"These were in the movie, *The Way*, too," Rachel said, and we took pictures of ourselves standing next to the sign.

Realizing how the French shops are only open from 9 to noon and 2 to 7 pm, and restaurants close at 2 pm then open again later, at 7 or 8 pm, we found a place for lunch at around 1 o'clock. Le Gourmandisos Amalxi served us an amazing salad with cheese, eggs, beets, and lettuce, with a ham and cheese patty on top. In France and Spain, I found the salads very nutritious, creative, delicious, hearty, and appealing, unlike so many ordinary salads I am served in the States. I also loved the bread and cheese, which never upset my stomach as they do at home. I'm not sure why the cheese is more digestible. My guess is it's all made locally and has no added preservatives. I know that American wheat is higher in gluten because it comes from hard red wheat, which is higher in protein and gluten. According to a friend, Julia Child famously lamented trying to make French bread with American flour.

Before heading back to our rooms, we walked to the edge of town so we could see where the trail began. Then we bought ham and cheese sandwiches on crusty, thick French bread at a shop so we would have something to eat if we didn't want to wait until 7 or 8 o'clock. We went into a few shops and befriended one shop owner, who had sold his pottery there for many years. I took his picture and couldn't resist capturing a group of children eating blue ice cream in cones outside under an arch. Then we walked back to our rooms to rest until 6:30 pm.

When we went back to the first restaurant for dinner, hoping to find the same hospitable waiter who had served us Basque burgers and beer the day before, another younger waiter apprehended us before we could sit down. Seeing us carrying our bagged sandwiches, he told us that we had to sit in another area if we weren't going to order food. We went to the another side of the restaurant to join others sitting at tables outside sipping wine and beer. We got two glasses of Sangria to go with our sandwiches.

A St. Jean Pied de Port restaurant

As we savored our bread and cheese sandwiches, Rachel shared memories of her dad and how, before he died, he'd told her an unbelievable story of how, while in the Navy, he helped others escape from a burning ship during World War II. I appreciated her willingness to tell me this account that obviously meant a lot to her. And I could see in her eyes, as she recounted the details, her own hope to make a difference in the lives of others. Maybe even help encourage or sustain a life one day, as her dad had. That was my hope too.

At 8:30 pm, we trudged back up Rue de la Citadelle to Hotel Ramuntcho and our waiting beds.

"Lord, thanks for this day. And bless tomorrow," I wrote in my journal. I thought again of the woman's response at the Pilgrim's Office and how unconcerned she was about the forecast. My weather app predicted heavy rain later the next day. And I wondered again what we would face. Rachel was determined to go over the Pyrenees. I would see how it went.

"We're going to need Your help, God!" I prayed as I slid beneath the covers.

STEP FOUR

A ROUGH TRUDGE TO RONCEVALLES

"No enterprise is too difficult to accomplish as long as you take it slowly. Take one small step after another and constantly keep your main objective in sight."

—Sanjiva Wijesinha in **Strangers on the Camino**

May 9th. Tuesday. Distance to Roncevalles, 14.9 miles. The first day of our trek. We met in the lobby at 6:30 am and walked in the half-light as the sun gradually peeked out from behind the mountains. As we marched down Rue de la Citadelle for the last time, we could see other trekkers already ahead of us. We joined the procession as we passed through the Porte d'Espagne and proceeded up an asphalt road. Since we'd opted for the harder route over the mountains, the way progressed steadily uphill.

As we went, the number of people ahead of us and behind us grew in number as more and more pilgrims joined us. And we began to realize that what began as our own unique trek was quickly evolving into an expanding and all-encompassing journey that we were a part of. And, somehow, the lives of many different people from all over the world were becoming intertwined with ours.

It started out as a nice day. There were a few wispy clouds overhead as we trudged for miles up the road past country houses and farms. We followed the signs, which were consistent at every turn, with a yellow arrow and a Camino shell over a blue background. They eventually led us off the road and up a dirt and rock-filled trail. Now, the incline was abruptly steeper. We both struggled with this more rugged and strenuous climb. I slowed down as others passed me by.

The trail up into the Pyrenees

The higher we climbed, the more spectacular the views became. Near the top of one steep hill, I found two older women sitting on a rock ledge beside the trail. Perched side by side, they enjoyed their sandwiches while appreciating the view below. From eastern Europe, they spoke no English, but motioned for me to sit down between them. I happily took them up on their offer to rest my feet for a few minutes as I waited for Rachel to make her way uphill. I pulled out a protein bar I'd stuck in my backpack and munched on that for a few minutes. When she drew closer, we moved over and invited her to sit with us, but she declined. She wanted to catch her breath, she said, so I took my time and finished my bar. An older Swedish woman walked past and cheerfully greeted us. "Bien Camino!" we all said in unison.

On the French side of the Pyrenees, pilgrims greet each other with "Bien Camino!" When we crossed over into Spain, the salute became "Buen Camino!" Either way, I was touched by each person who took the time to hail me. Some trekkers embraced the journey in a serious way and walked with their head down to contemplate each step. Other, more gregarious pilgrims brought joy to the journey and greeted each person heartily along the way. A few people thought of it as a celebration to be shared with everyone by way of loud music. One young Spaniard carried a boom box on his shoulder all the way up the first mountain and blasted his favorite tunes out to all his fellow trekkers. I watched the faces of others near me as he passed by, and I could tell that they felt the same way I did. Most of us just wanted to escape civilization's blasts and appreciate the peaceful, natural sights and sounds around us. I forgave him when I realized that he was walking the Camino with his mother, who waited for him at the top of the mountain. I saw them together hugging when he joined her, and my heart was glad. But my insides ached a little when I thought about how much it would have meant to me and my son to experience this journey together.

Away from the urban blare of lights, loud voices, and traffic, I silently appreciated the climb with its wonderful valley views of flower-covered meadows, sheep-filled pastures, green spring-leafed trees, and white-washed farmhouses that grew smaller as we climbed higher. In the distance, we could always see the deep-blue mountains whose peeks were touched by a purple-hued sky.

"Awesome!" I thought.

I enjoyed the rural sounds more and more as I progressed. Many fences were so close to us that we could reach over and pet the sheep that grazed on the other side. Some bleated at us as if to say, "Move along, pilgrim!" I also appreciated the birds that soared above me and I tried to identify as many of their calls as I could while walking.

Sheep along the trail

All of us grew more intent as we huffed and puffed farther up the rocky trail that led from one new mountain to the next. When we saw a bend ahead, we all hoped it was the final summit, but we sighed when we saw another steep hill around the corner. The uphill climb seemed to never end. We'd expected a café in Hunto, a settlement on the road before we reached the rocky trail. The blond woman at the Pilgrim's Office had told us to expect to get coffee there. But, when we passed by the small group of buildings, we could see that nothing was open. So, we kept walking, wishing we had been able to enjoy a nice, hot cup of coffee and rest our feet for at least a few minutes. Even a few miles out, we felt like we'd been walking for hours.

Finally, almost five miles up, we approached Orisson, still in France, which was no more than a stone-faced building with brown shutters that housed a restaurant and an albergue. Rachel recognized the building from *The Way*. One scene in the movie showed Tom sitting at one of the picnic tables that sat in front. We were never so happy to stand in line with other trekkers for a cup of coffee! I also ordered a thick, half-loaf of French bread with ham and cheese stuffed inside. As we sat at the wooden tables inside, Rachel looked at me with tears in her eyes, and I could tell she was already spent. She was enduring unspoken pain in her hips and knees. Somehow my joints seemed to be holding up better than I expected. In spite of the sighs and tears, neither of us really wanted to turn back. Though we weren't sure what the rest of the day's trek might entail, we agreed that we had to somehow reach our next destination.

"We can do this!" I said hopefully, while clenching my teeth and fists.

The fountain and albergue in Orisson

We rested for a while then crossed the road to fill our water bottles with pure mountain water from a streaming fountain. As we set out from Orisson, the road we walked was a bit more level and paved, and we were thankful. We looked behind us and noticed the clouds above the distant mountains growing darker and more sinister-looking. And they were moving toward us. When we gazed ahead, we didn't see as many pilgrims as we'd seen coming up the mountain. And the number of walkers gradually thinned out the farther we walked so that we ended up being the only two trekkers along the path.

We passed many fields, some sheep, and occasional cairns—piles of stones left by passersby—covered with notes and memorabilia. But, as the clouds moved in, bringing with them rain, then freezing sleet, forceful winds, and fog, our vision was so obscured that all we could see was a few feet in front of us. At one point, I turned around and could barely see Rachel behind me, waving her hiking pole to get my attention. I was beginning to understand how Tom's son might have died on this stretch of the Camino. I remember seeing a truck parked in the grass coming slowly into view and then a man standing with his dog and wearing a black beret. And, finally, the herd of sheep they guarded became clearer the closer we got. As we rounded one hill, we were surprised to see horses grazing beside the road, but almost hidden by the blinding fog.

A horse barely visible in the thick fog

We scrupulously watched for Camino signs to make sure we were going the right way. When we reached one bend, the road went one way, to the left, and a dirt trail went off another way, up and over a hill to the right. Rachel was convinced that the woman at the Pilgrim's Office had said to take the trail, which went past a weathervane and a solar panel. The

Camino signs did seem to point this way, so I followed her, but soon realized and commented on how treacherous and precarious the trail looked as it quickly descended from a dirt path down a steep decline of rocks. The instability of the trail grew more obvious as it became increasingly slippery from the rain and sleet. As I groped for security, moving from stone to stone and trying to steady myself with my poles, I finally slid the rest of the way down into a thick, feet-deep layer of deteriorating leaves that covered the path at the bottom. My feet sank ankle-deep into the sludge that reminded me of mounds of milk-soaked raisin bran, and I fell over into the mess, becoming covered from chest to toe with the soggy muck. I pushed myself up, bracing against the stones that led uphill, and tried to make my way in my now-soaked, leaf-plastered, "waterproof" shoes. But I sank deeper and deeper with each step as I made my way through a darkening forest.

I felt like I was the main character in an ominous thriller where the victim is never seen again alive. The haze was so intense that I could only make out what was right in front of me—a sludge-filled path that went on and on and descended down and down. Beside me, a steep cliff with hovering trees fell away down the fog-covered mountain. We walked mile after mile through this murky muck and mire. There were no signs of a life anywhere, and I began to worry and wonder if we were on the right trail. Had anyone walked this way lately? It didn't seem so. At least for many years. A few landmarks like an ancient fountain with an engraving that read *Fontaine de Roland* and seashells decorating the base seemed to indicate that some pilgrims might have walked this path many years ago. I discovered later that this fountain commemorated an event in 778. It was where the Basques ambushed and wiped out part of Charlemagne's army as they came across the mountains to Aquitaine after they'd fought the Muslims in Spain and ravaged several towns. Roland was a skilled and bold warrior in Charlemagne's court, and he was renowned as a chivalrous role model for knights.

A fountain along the wooded trail to Roncevalles

I found out later that most pilgrims opt for the road route to Roncevalles instead of this less-traveled, sluggish, and neglected path. We grew more and more concerned as the hours ticked by. When I looked at my watch and saw it was 7:20 pm, I grew alarmed.

"I hope we make it out of here before dark!" I yelled back at Rachel, who was making her way down another steep, rocky decline. She carefully stepped from one rock to another, trying to balance herself with her poles, just as I had done.

"Oh, we have plenty of time!" she responded. But, when she checked her watch and saw the time, she too grew very concerned.

There was no end in sight, and we trudged on through the decaying leaves. I prayed for some verification that we were on the right path. Then I looked behind me to see two pilgrims approaching us. As they zoomed past, they both yelled "Bien Camino!" and I thanked God for this reassurance that we weren't lost forever in this mucky "mire land." After a while I saw a clearing ahead. A road crossed the trail and a sign on the other side read, "Roncesvalles, .5 km." with an arrow pointing right.

"Yay!" I gasped under my breath. "Thanks, God!"

We turned and followed the road and soon rounded a bend to see a group of buildings ahead. As we approached, not knowing which way to go to find our hotel, we saw a backpacker walking toward us. We asked him if he knew where we were and which way to our hotel, Casa Beneficiados. He indicated that, if we went around the buildings to the left, and then turned right, we'd see what there was of Roncevalles. It was 8:30 pm.

Roncesvalles, in the region of Navarre, is a small village of 21 people situated on the Urrobi River at an altitude of 3,000 feet. It is 2.5 miles from the French border, but 13 miles through mountainous roads. As we walked past one old stone building with brown shutters and a sign that said, *La Posada*, we noticed a few people standing outside the door smoking. They waved to us and yelled "Buen Camino!" It looked like a restaurant. Rachel recognized it from one scene in *The Way*.

We found our hotel beyond a church and behind some buildings along this main road, and we traipsed in, tracking leaves, mud, and debris with each step. The hotel staff was welcoming. I guessed they'd seen this before, but we still felt badly that we were so covered with crud. We located the office to check in, and a young woman there told us that Tee Travel, who contracted with Mac's to transport our luggage, had grown very concerned that we had not arrived. We told her all that we'd been through, and she suggested we call Mac's and let them know we were ok.

After checking in and getting our passports stamped, we trudged up some stairs to our rooms, which were spacious, neat, and clean. I had two rooms; one included a couch with a coffee table, a table with chairs, and a small kitchen area with a refrigerator, a sink with a counter, a microwave, and a coffeemaker. The other was a bedroom with plenty of shelves and closet space and an attached bathroom. I quickly pulled off my wet, soggy, debris-covered clothes and shoes, washed them off the best I could in the kitchen sink and lay them out to dry on the table. Then I took a shower. As I stood under the warm water, I muttered another prayer.

"Thank You, God, for getting us here safely!"

I was also grateful as I unpacked the dry clothes and the other pair of hiking shoes I'd brought from my suitcase that had arrived safely.

At 9:30 pm, Rachel and I met in the lobby to try to find something to eat. We were famished. But we quickly found out that all the restaurants were closed. We went next door to a bar that was still open and sat at a counter. We ordered Riojas and drank two glasses each, along with the only available food: potato chips, muffins, and croissants. As we guzzled the wine, thankful to have some nourishment, we bantered with the bartender, Johnny, who clowned around with us and appreciated our attention. We told him about how we'd just survived the first day of the Camino, barely making it over the Pyrenees from St. Jean Pied de Port.

"It only took us 14 hours!" we exclaimed.

But, seriously, we were thankful beyond words that we had actually survived to tell the story! It had definitely proved to be more challenging than I could have imagined, testing me in all categories: mentally, physically, and spiritually. But we'd made it! I sighed and wondered if we could do what was needed to make it to our next destination. If this was just the first day, what would the next two weeks be like? I slunk down on the barstool as I sipped my Rioja.

A signpost along the Camino trail over the Pyrenees

STEP FIVE

ALEE AKERRETA

"Some purists consider it anathema to distract themselves from what the Camino might be telling them at any given moment. But with a mind that loops and gets caught in eddies more often than I'd care for anyway, I've come to regard my own process as not so precious. There are as many paths to purification as there are walkers along the road. I'll take whatever help I can get on a blistering afternoon."

—Andrew McCarthy in **Walking with Sam**

May 10th. Wednesday. Distance to Akerreta, 17.1 miles. 6 am. I woke up and jumped out of bed. Even though we were up until 11 pm the night before, I was ready to go. I got dressed and went down for breakfast at 7 am. The room set aside for pilgrims to dine was already in full swing, and I was shown to a table for two in an adjoining room. I texted Rachel that I was downstairs then went outside the dining area into the lobby to meet her and show her where I was sitting, since I knew it would be hard for her to find me in the hidden room. She came, I showed her the table, and we went to help ourselves to the usual spread, with the addition of different kinds of cereal.

At the coffee maker, I had to select the size of cup and type of coffee I wanted and whether or not I wanted milk in it. It was so complicated that a person next to me had to show me how to work it. As I stood with Rachel, making my second cup, we began to converse with a couple who were waiting to make their own personalized cups of coffee. The man's name was Philip, my son's name. He even spelled it the same way. He was from England and was traveling with Thais from South America. We shared our many challenges in making our way over the Pyrenees and how long it had taken us. Philip talked about trusting in God for the journey and, as he did, I noticed a cross hanging around his neck. His few words encouraged me immensely and were another affirmation of success on the journey and a reminder of how God had gotten us here safely.

We went back to our rooms and met again around 10 am in the lobby to walk around the town. We had already decided not to trek the whole distance to our next destination, Akerreta, so we would also need to figure out how to get a taxi. Our "waterproof" shoes were still soaking wet, as were some of our clothes, the weather looked precarious with a chance of rain again, and Rachel's knees and hips were still sore from our first day's slog. Miraculously, mine were doing ok. I had no lingering pains...so far.

As we walked through the small area that made up Roncevalles, we ventured into a beautiful Gothic-style cathedral, the Colegiata de Santa Maria, which was built to imitate the Nôtre Dame Cathedral in Paris. Looking up as I entered, I was awed by the domed roof with supporting veins made of stone that arched up to a central point on the ceiling. In the front, a long, white-cloth-covered table stood under a canopy with a circle of lights shining down on it. And a golden Madonna standing on a gold octagonal pedestal held the Christ child, flanked by two gilded angels holding candles. They were surrounded by spectacular stained-glass windows that reached up to the ceiling.

"King Sancho VII built this church in the 13th century as part of the hospital's facilities in Roncesvalles," according to *spain.info*. "Its purpose was to provide succour to pilgrims on the Way of Saint James after crossing the Pyrenees." The church's highlights include the cloister, the chapels of San Agustín and Santiago, and the crypt. Its mural paintings date back to the 13th century, and its art treasures include a collection of precious metalwork and a chess set belonging to Charlemagne.

We walked back toward the hotel, past La Posada and an impressive stone monument commemorating The Battle of Roncevaux Pass, which involved Roland and Charlemagne's army in the high mountain pass that bordered France and Spain.

A monument to commemorate The Battle of Roncevaux Pass

We ran into three people we'd met on the trail the day before from Texas and Portland, Oregon. They recognized us, and we ended up telling them about our challenges getting over the Pyrenees. They couldn't believe how long it had taken us. They'd arrived in Roncevalles by 5:30 the day before, in time to go to a Pilgrim's Mass at the cathedral! We shared our plan to take a taxi partway to Akerreta, and they pointed to a cab parked nearby and said it had driven them there from another town that day. The driver,

Mikkal, was sitting in the bar now. We went and found him drinking coffee and talking to Johnny. He agreed to drive us as far as Larrasoaña, which was about 17 miles away. We had chosen this town because a map indicated that there was a pharmacy, where Rachel could get more ibuprofen, and a café where we could stop and get another cup of coffee. It was within a mile of Akerreta. So, we ran back to the hotel to gather up our belongings and meet Mikkal at his van.

On the drive to Larrasoaña, we went up and down many hilly miles and realized how many steep climbs we'd avoided that day. We were relieved. Mikkal dropped us off in the tiny town, and we realized quickly that there was no pharmacy or café here. So, we picked up the trail near a bridge, and, as we crossed over, we ran into a woman from Hamburg, Germany, who confirmed that there was no drugstore here. Rachel told her what she needed, and the woman dug through her backpack to produce enough ibuprofen to get her through until she could buy more. We were so thankful to have met her. Another God-send, I thought.

The path from Larrasoaña to Akerreta was lined with lovely trees and, beyond these, meadows filled with flowers. We arrived around noon and found Hotel Akerreta. The tiny hamlet, with only 11 inhabitants as of 2020, is located in the Esteribar Valley, near the Rio Arga. Once a place of royal lordship with about six families, it was organized around a medieval church called La Transfiguración and has a few buildings, including an albergue and some mountain-style homes where the masonry stone corners contrast with the plaster on the rest of the façade.

The door to our hotel was locked. We knocked repeatedly, but no one answered. Somewhat frustrated, we decided to sit in chairs outside on a patio until someone showed up and opened the door. Rachel recognized the hotel and the patio area from *The Way* and swore there were scenes filmed right here. I didn't remember them exactly. But I'd only seen the movie twice. She'd seen it many times.

Not long after we settled down, a van pulled up and a young man hopped out and opened the back to pull out luggage that was being transported here. He spoke English, so we asked if he could find out when the hotel opened. He went to a side door, someone let him in, and he returned to tell us the owner would open at 2 pm. Our only concern was that dark clouds were hovering overhead.

"Great!" I muttered. We had no choice but to sit and wait, even if we got soaked in the process.

Hotel Akerrata's charming facade

The time flew by as we checked messages and talked. Finally, just at 2 pm, the owner, Joseph, nonchalantly opened a front door and we went in. He verified that his hotel had been highlighted in *The Way*, and he told us how it had taken the producers over a week to film the needed scenes. He also showed us where part of the front-facing balcony had been burned black by a fire started by a woman who placed candles outside her door for "ambience." He was still trying to replace the wood that had been blackened only two weeks ago. It made me sad to think of him having to redo part of such an historically beautiful façade. His hotel was built in the 17th century.

My room, number 21, was on the second floor, and I was captivated by my view from a door that led onto my own section of the balcony, which was only two doors down from the burnt area. The interior was simple, with a single bed, desk and chair, wardrobe, and clean but small bathroom with a tiny, curtained window. But the balconied vista was spectacular. I could gaze out and see beyond Arreketa to green pastures full of horses bearing large, swinging, jangling bells around their necks. Beyond them, flowering meadows, trees, and forest-covered mountains created an enthralling scene. The day was cool and pleasant, and the rain had passed us by, so I enjoyed standing outside, breathing in the fresh air, and watching the intermittent clouds and sunshine. I could hover there for hours, but my first order of business was to bag up all the wet and dirty clothes that were stuffed into my suitcase, which had arrived safely, and take them down to Joseph. He would have someone do my laundry so I could pick it up early the next morning.

The door to my outdoor balcony

Dinner was at 8 pm, so, once I'd delivered the sopping clothes, I took this time to rest and read. I perused more of a book I was enjoying called *The Awe of God* by John Bevere. I made notes in my journal, "I am touched by Bevere's advice when a coworker sees you through critical eyes. This advice is great for anyone: 'Refrain from sharing the intimate secrets of your heart with any employee (or person) until you know they are established....' When people are cursed with 'critical eyes,' we must keep them at a distance until we know that we can trust them with our hearts."

I also wrote down a quote from Lisa Terkeurst's book, *Good Boundaries and Goodbyes*, which I read on the plane from Atlanta: "Access requires responsibility." And I thought of struggles I'd faced in my own family and at work when people did not choose to see me as I am, but as they chose to see me...as a reflection of their own challenges with others who treated them unkindly or as a reminder of their own misperceptions or failures. My mind flipped back to the days before my son's death and the way some family members had seen me...very critically. Then I prayed for my own healing from the hurt they'd caused me and any latent hatred that remained in their hearts as a root of bitterness. This weight was one of the mental burdens I had carried for quite a while that I longed to lay down, with His help. I asked God then for His hand of protection on my heart going forward and for a complete release from my tendency to take things so personally. When I reflected on this request later, I realized how unusually open-hearted, generous, and kind were the people I met on the Camino. This, in itself, was very healing for me and helped me to attain the release I sought in this area.

"Tomorrow, it looks like rain," I wrote with a sigh, then jotted down a prayer. "Lord, help us make our way successfully, and show us what will work out best. My shoes are still very wet!"

After spending time considering what I was learning on this trip, I decided to go downstairs a little early and scrounge up a glass of wine. It was 7:30, and I was greeted at the bottom of the stairs, near the entry, by a couple from Ireland and a man named John from Seattle. We chatted for a few minutes while I waited for Joseph, who brought me two glasses of wine. I took one up to Rachel, and she showed me her room. It was small, like mine, and, instead of a door to a balcony, it had a window with a wonderful view of the meadows beyond Arreketa. She happily took the glass of wine.

We met downstairs closer to 8 and sat on a couch in a sitting area just off the entryway. A couple from Germany settled onto another couch next to us, the Irish couple I'd met earlier stepped inside the door and greeted us, and an older man sat alone at a small table near the window. As some of us discussed our experiences on the Camino, I looked around and wondered how many countries were represented in this tiny hotel. When it was time, we all walked into a small dining room attached to the sitting area. Rachel and I were joined at a table for four by John and his friend, Carole, from Florida. When all the lodgers were seated, Joseph began to bring in beautiful salads filled with white asparagus, ripe red tomatoes, delicious green olives, and fresh lettuce, which we topped with a typically European vinegar and oil dressing. After this came homemade beef stew marinated in red wine, followed by Spanish flan with berry sauce. All of this was accompanied by plenty of delicious Spanish red wine, and we sighed with pleasure as we shared our experiences and wondered what the next day's adventures would bring us.

Before I dozed off that night, I uttered my thanks for the pleasant accommodations, the good food, and our new friends. But I wondered how far we'd be able to walk the next day and what the weather would be like. I looked over at my still-wet shoes and sighed. Hopefully we would not encounter more rain...yet.

STEP SIX

OLE! PAMPLONA

"Remember, the Camino gives you what you need, not necessarily what you want. The trick, then, is not to wish you had something else, but rather to find the benefit, the lesson, the opportunity for growth in what you have. When that is your goal, you never have to ask, 'Now what?'"

—*Gordon J. Bernhardt in* **Buen Camino**

May 11th. Thursday. Distance to Pamplona, 9.9 miles. I stepped onto my balcony at 5:50 am and was relieved to see no sign of rain-bearing clouds. Then I checked my shoes, which I'd placed outside. They were dry! "Yay!" I muttered to myself. I took my suitcase down at 7:30, since Joseph had said they should be placed in the lobby by 8 am, then asked Joseph to fill up my thermos with coffee. As I waited for him to return, I wandered into the sitting area and found the man I'd seen the night before sitting alone. He rested an elbow on a small, round table and sipped a cup of coffee as he gazed intently out the window. My eyes followed his and I, too, was drawn to the sunrise view. The window, dissected by a wooden grille in the shape of a cross, held four paneled pictures: the bottom two showed glimpses of red-flowered vines that crept into view as they embraced the panels; the top two captured a distant, green pasture surrounded by forested mountains capped by purple and pink-tinged clouds.

"Beautiful!" I whispered as I turned toward him. "Where are you from?" I ventured.

"Madrid," he said.

I told him where I was from, and he mentioned that his son had studied chemical engineering at the University of Texas.

"My parents went to school there," I said, thinking, "Small world."

When I asked where his son worked now, he explained that he was somewhere in Europe. His answer was vague, and he seemed hesitant to go into any detail, so I didn't press him with more questions. I wondered if he'd fallen out with his son, or, like me, maybe his son was deceased, and he was offering this pilgrimage as a memorial to him. I would never know, but my heart hurt for him because of the sadness I sensed.

I remembered the days, weeks, months, and years after my son died and how my heart hurt constantly. I had little relief for at least two years. Many memories would send me spiraling down into a grief-filled abyss: a song that reminded me of him, a red truck that looked like his, photos of him I'd kept on my phone or in an album, his children who reminded me of him, a letter or picture he'd kept, drawings from his childhood I'd saved.... Often it would take a good amount of time for me to claw my way back out of these dark pits. Whenever I met or saw a young man who reminded me of Phil, I'd stop and talk to him. Sometimes I'd tell him that God's hand was on him because I sensed that. Many responded that they were touched and appreciated my confirming words.

Not too long ago, I was able to look through the picture albums again, and my heart was elated to see how happy Phil had been as a child. He was always smiling and sunny. But then, when he was a teen, the days grew much cloudier. He seemed to experience some depression. But somehow, we got through those days together. Once he entered his 20s and found new, more encouraging friendships and an undeniable faith, his life changed, and he became his joyful self again. Thank God, these were the years he ended with before he lost his breath.

I stood next to the man from Madrid and gazed with him out the window at the fabulous view, and I prayed silently for him and his son. Rachel, who'd texted that she'd meet me downstairs at 7:35, bounded down the steps and entered the sitting room, and we made our way to the dining room to sit with John and Carole again. We enjoyed another European-style breakfast, but, this time, along with the fresh juice. coffee, butter, and jam, our plates held only one very large croissant. John rolled his eyes and later complained about the sparsity of food. We didn't say anything.

We returned to our rooms to gather our backpacks and meet downstairs. I found Rachel outside talking to John, who stood in front waiting for a friend named Mark to join him from another hotel so they could walk together. We said goodbye, after making sure we had his contact information so we could hook up with him again. Then we set out down a tree-lined path for Pamplona. Not even a mile into our walk, John and Mark bounded past us down the trail. Even as we walked slowly, I could tell, only a few miles in, that Rachel was in pain. We stopped in one café along the way and enjoyed a cup of café con leche. Even though we had to wait in line to order and sit with others we didn't know, the reprieve was welcome.

As we continued to walk, I realized my urgent need for a restroom and spotted one below the road in a park, so I jostled through bushes down a steep, narrow path that led to a humble building with a sign that

I recognized as being a public restroom. As I approached the facility, I wondered what I'd find, since I was never sure what to expect in European bathrooms. In some, you might have to pay to use the facility; others are co-ed; and, in some, you might find a toilet, a bidet, or a hole in the floor. I was the only person inside and found what I needed without too much trouble. Thank God, there was a toilet, and it was working and clean. I used it quickly, exited the building, and scrambled back up the hill to join Rachel.

Farther down the trail, we met a man from the States who had walked the Camino many times. Our conversation was short; he moved ahead quickly, and we crossed a stream alone. We came to a park and the entrance to a steep climb that went up the side of a mountain. It looked foreboding. A van sat on a road next to the park, and a man paced back and forth beside it. I could tell that Rachel was hesitant to climb the mountainous path, and I asked the man if we could get a ride with him. He was waiting to pick up a group of hikers and couldn't accommodate us but told us about another more level trail that led to Pamplona just around the corner. We were thankful for his suggestion.

Along the paved trail, we ran into a woman who sat on a bench dressing her blistered feet. We sat with her for a while, and she told us her story of walking the Camino alone. She thanked us for offering our help, but she had done this before, and she knew what it took and how to stop and "take care of things" along the way. We went on, and, as we approached Pamplona, it became harder to discern the signs along the busy streets. As we turned one corner, having walked about five miles, Rachel accidentally stepped off the sidewalk and fell. I helped her up and knew we had to find a ride from here, first because she had turned her ankle and second because we were unsure which way to go.

I turned around and saw a man sitting at a picnic table in front of a bar smoking. I walked back, sat down at the table, and said, "Taxi?" He pulled up an app on his phone with a number to call and handed me the phone. I tried to explain that I didn't speak Spanish and handed the phone back to him.

"You call for us?" I asked and pointed at him.

He understood and called for a cab, giving the person our location, which I did not know. When it arrived, he went over to the female driver and told her where to take us, since I'd told him the name of the hotel. After we put our packs and poles in the back of the car, we gratefully opened the doors and slid in.

"Thanks, God!" I sighed, wondering if the man was an angel in disguise.

The whole incident reminded me of something my son had taught me about "serendipity" and trusting that God would always provide a way when there seemed to be no way. He was an example of this himself, since he'd moved on his own to Denver after graduating from high school and found a group of fast friends who supported and encouraged him. He progressed from being a struggling teen who was jailed twice for stealing cigarettes and possessing marijuana to a responsible young man with his own window-washing business. I was so proud of him and what he'd accomplished! He was never afraid to venture out and meet new people and help them redirect their own lives as others had helped him rebuild his.

Our taxi driver sped the remaining four or five miles through crowded streets, and I grew more and more grateful that we hadn't tried to walk through this maze of streets and signs. She pulled up in front of Hotel Tres Reyes (Spanish for "Three Kings") on Jardines de la Taconera street, and our jaws dropped. It was a beautiful 11-story hotel in the middle of the city, close to all the sites.

"At least four stars," I said.

We arrived around 1 pm and checking in was a delight because everyone at the desk spoke English. Their hospitable attitudes and smiles made us feel welcome, and we were relieved to be here. Our luggage had arrived, and we went immediately up to our rooms, which were ready! Mine was just as amazing as the lavishly aesthetic lobby. It was very spacious, with contemporary furniture, including a swervy, comfortable chair to read in, beautiful lamps to give just the right amount of light, and a large, king-sized bed. I knew Rachel would be thrilled since she didn't like feeling cramped in the narrow single beds we'd put up with in St. Jean and Akerreta. The bathroom was also large and clean and new with a sparkling white sink and walk-in shower. I showered, changed, and then met Rachel downstairs in the lobby at 3 pm to go out. Thankfully, her ankle seemed to be holding up.

Sitting in the foothills of the Pyrenees, Pamplona was named for Pompey the Great, a Roman military leader who founded the city in 68 BCE. It was the capital of Navarre from the 11th century until 1841. Once a medieval Basque kingdom, it was annexed by Castile, the "Land of Castles," a kingdom under which Spain was united in the late 15th and early 16th centuries that is dotted with remote villages. Pamplona, the largest, with a population of about 191,000 as of 2003, is best known for the *Festival of San Fermin* every July and the *Running of the Bulls.*

In his book, *Two Million Steps*, Patrick DeVaney writes: "San Fermin (Saint Fermin), the son of a Roman senator, was reared near here and is the patron saint of Pamplona. He was martyred in 303 because of his faith. One story relates that he was beheaded in France while another more popular version claims that he died as a result of being dragged through the streets of Amiens, France, as bulls chased him. Such is the origin of the *Running of the Bulls.*

"The festival stretches for eight days and starts with setting off the *chupinazo* (a rocket) from the balcony of city hall on July 6. The next day, a huge procession including politicians, pilgrims, and religious dignitaries carry the fifteenth-century statue of Saint Fermin through the town. Big-headed papier-mâché puppets called *gigantes* also dance in the street to honor the saint. The *Running of the Bulls* occurs early in the morning and can be very dangerous. Many runners (*mozos*) are gored and trampled, and there have been several deaths over the years. It takes two to three minutes for the bulls to run the course, but it takes much longer for the *mozos* to prepare for the run. It seems that a great deal of the preparation starts at the local bars the night before and goes all night long leading up to the run."

We first found a place to eat close by on San Nicolas Street. The door was open to Bar Otano, so we peeked inside. A few tables with benches sat along one wall and a bar with stools beckoned to us next to the entrance. Delicious-looking plates full of bite-sized appetizers called tapas, or pintxos in northern Spain, sat on the counter, and we knew we'd found the right place. The waitress brought us large glasses of Rioja, some tasty pintxos, and wonderful salads piled high with olives, tuna, white asparagus, toma-toes, lettuce, and anchovies. Delicious!

After gorging ourselves on these delights, we made our way toward Plaza del Castillo, in the heart of Pamplona. I had read that this was Ernest Hemingway's first stop when he arrived in Pamplona in July 1923. He made this plaza his "hot spot" while in the city. We found a pharmacy on a corner so Rachel could get some salves to treat her knees and ankle, then we made our way to the bust of Ernest Hemingway, which sat in front of the bullfighting ring on Plaza del Toro.

We walked up to the entrance and signed up for a tour of the ring, which I'd wanted to see since reading Hemingway's book, *The Sun Also Rises*, years ago. I was fascinated by the novel, which he wrote in 1926, and how he described the American and British expatriates who walked along the Camino de Santiago from Paris to Pamplona to participate in the *Running of the Bulls* and the bullfights. Looking back, I think his book sparked an interest in the Camino even before I saw *The Way*.

I had another revelation when I read King Solomon's book of Ecclesi-astes in the Bible later and came across these verses: *"One generation passes away, and another generation comes; but the earth abides forever. The sun also rises, and the sun goes down, and hastens to the place where it arose."* Hemingway's book title came from this passage! I was curious to discover the reason why he thought these words were significant and, the more I read, the more I understood that he was experiencing, along with others, the terrible after-effects of World War I. Despite this, he still believed that the "Lost Generation," or those who were considered to be decadent, dissolute, and irretrievably damaged by World War I, was in fact resilient and strong.

Ernest Hemingway's bust in Pamplona

Many people today look at the youth and think they are "going to hell in a handbasket." Those I met along the trail, however, impressed me very differently. Giving me great hope for the next generation, I saw how many of them are seeking something deeper, something more meaningful.

In his book, Hemingway investigated "the themes of love and death, the revivifying power of nature and the concept of masculinity" (*Wikipedia*). He converted to Catholicism while writing *The Sun Also Rises*, and I could relate to his desire for greater spirituality and his feeling of revitalizing power from experiencing nature as I walked the Camino.

Solomon, like Hemingway, thought that people's strivings, like fighting in a war or running with the bulls, are often fruitless, and what we leave behind is often forgotten. He saw the meaninglessness of our efforts, which are usually expended to impress others, yet how others forget who we were after we are gone. And who inherits all we have struggled so hard to achieve? Often people with no appreciation for all we've done! So sad. But, Solomon concluded, God promises it will all benefit those He loves. "That is my hope, Lord!" I wrote in my journal later that day.

We were ushered into the bullfighting ring with audio guides to help us make our way around the arena and its adjacent rooms, where the bulls and bullfighters gathered. We watched a group of young people in the ring pretending like they were toreadors prancing around a make-believe bull. As we walked out of the ring, we ran into a man from Australia named Ricardo who was there with his wife and was also walking on the Camino. His wife gave us an invitation to a Pilgrim's Mass at a cathedral in town that evening. But, after walking back through Plaza del Castillo and up Santo Domingo Street, where the *Running of the Bulls* takes place each July, and after seeing a large statue honoring the event, we made our way back to Tres Reyes along San Nicolas Street. It was close to 5 pm and we were ready to relax.

A Pamplona monument to honor the Running of the Bulls

The hotel's lobby was so inviting that we decided to climb to the top of some carpeted stairs that led to a lounge and a bar. We sat in very comfortable chairs and ordered Old Fashioneds and munchies. It wasn't time for dinner to be served, but a kind waiter brought us a large variety of nuts, olives, breadsticks, cheese, and crackers. And that was all we needed.

We rested, talked, and looked around the lounge, which was decorated with beautiful glass chandeliers, a purple-lit tree, and one wall of stained glass—an artistic rendition of three kings, who were holding hands. It reminded me of the Trinity: the Father, Son, and Holy Spirit, but later I learned that the people of Spain highly venerate the three kings, or wise men, who came to visit the baby Jesus as described in the Bible, and they dedicate a special day to memorialize their visit. On January 5th every year, parades take place throughout the country to celebrate the arrival of the kings. Spanish families line the streets of their hometown to get a glimpse of the cabalgata de los reyes mago, or Three Kings Day parade.

A group of people sat in comfortable chairs beneath the stained-glass mural and dutifully listened to a long-winded speaker, and we wondered if they were part of a Camino walking-group. A man in a bow tie and light-colored suit, who reminded me of Truman Capote, sat next to us and peered nervously toward the group. He jumped up when the meeting ended, and the attendees disseminated down the steps. He ran to greet one man who was leaving, and it was obvious that he'd been watching and waiting for him. We sat there, curiously wondering about their relationship while enjoying our drinks and snacks. And we were very thankful we had nowhere to go at the moment.

Before retiring, I perused the maps and distances to our next stop, Puenta la Reina. The steep climb on the way to the top of a mountain, Alto del Perdon, which was midway along the trail, looked precarious, and I wondered if we could do it.

"Another challenging day ahead," I sighed and cringed. "Maybe another physical test for us." And I wondered if we were up for it.

STEP SEVEN

RENDEZVOUS IN PUENTA LA REINA

"There are moments when life seems to make the kind of sense we often wish it made—when the universe seems to sit in our lap, when things are revealed in a simplicity of being and unity. They are moments that add up to more than the sum of their parts—moments of serendipity when things come together in a meeting of circumstance, timing, and mood. It's impossible to predict or plan or fully explain such times. They defy efforts at repeating, even if all outward elements are the same. That they seem more common in travel than at home is one of the primary reasons people like me bother to go anywhere in the first place."

—*Andrew McCarthy in* **Walking with Sam**

May 12th. Friday. Distance to Puenta la Reina, 14.5 miles. With Rachel's ankle and knees still in a precarious state, we decided to take a taxi to the highest point of our journey between Pamplona and Puenta la Reina. After an amazing breakfast in Tres Reyes' large dining hall with counters full of choices that expanded even more on the typical bread, butter, jam, jamón (thin-sliced ham), cheese, cereal, yoghurt, fresh-squeezed juice, coffee, etc., we walked around the streets near the hotel and found a pharmacy and an ATM machine at a bank. Returning to the hotel, we discovered a street lined with statues of famous Spanish people. I took a few pictures, then we went back to our rooms, regrouped in the lobby, and had someone at the hotel call for a taxi.

We asked the driver, who spoke English, to take us to Alto del Perdon, or *The Mount of Forgiveness*. Some have described it as an enchanting rise over the plains of Navarre. On the way, our driver told us that most Spanish young men try to walk the Camino so they can put this accomplishment on their résumé. It makes them more eligible to get hired, he explained.

It reminded me of my son's "résumé" and how my mom had insisted that all her children and grandchildren go to college after high school. Of course, I was the black sheep of the family—the only child of her four that rebelled from this mandate and quit college in my sophomore year to get married. Mom had a fit at the time but was thrilled when her first grandchild arrived a year later. I did not return to college until I was in my 30s, when I needed to get more classroom cred so I could find a way to support myself, especially after I realized that my marriage would never be what I hoped it would. Phil was a pea from the same pod. After struggling to finish high school, and at my mom and my prompting, he started his first year at a community college, but didn't make it through the first semester. We quickly realized that this intelligent but ADHD-afflicted kid just couldn't comfortably sit still for hours in a classroom, and that he would never aspire to a desk job. Though his CV would never include hours of college classes and scholarly achievements, it would encompass many hours of hard work under an encouraging mentor and his own brand of ingenuity at building a business and doing research on topics he was interested in.

On the way to Alto del Perdon, we drove over and around many hills for about nine miles. We watched as raindrops splashed against the windshield and car windows, making streams out of resounding drops that oozed down together until they reached the bottom of each window. We prepared ourselves as best we could by pulling out our raingear before exiting the car and making sure to cover our backpacks with special rain-covers we'd brought with us.

The driver dropped us off at the summit, and we guiltily extracted ourselves and our bags from the warm car as many diehard pilgrims stood around us, shivering and enduring the cold wind and rain after trudging all the way up to the peak of the mountain. We were immediately struck by the huge wind turbines that whirled their white blades like whirligigs, trying to stir up the gray, overcast, cloudy sky from the tops of the surrounding mountains.

We walked across the road to see the famous steel sculpture called *Monument to the Pilgrims* that had graced the top of this mount since 1996. Twelve large characters that range from a few feet to 10 feet tall follow one after the other, and an inscription on the monument can be translated into *"Where the way of the wind meets that of the stars."* Recently I'd read a quote about the monument by Jean Mitchell-Lanham in her book, *The Lore of the Camino de Santiago:* "The sculpture exhibits a small history of pilgrims and the pilgrimage...through various stages of development, from the beginning in the Middle Ages up to the present day, in the form of a procession. Of the twelve pilgrims, the first pilgrim appears to be searching for the route and symbolizes the beginning of interest in the pilgrimage. Next is a group of three that depicts the growth or rise in popularity of the Camino...followed by another group depicted as merchants or tradesmen on horseback that symbolize the medieval era of merchants hawking their wares to the pilgrims. Spaced away from them is a solitary figure that characterizes the decline in pilgrimages due to political, religious, and social unrests from the mid-fourteenth to the mid-twentieth centuries. At the very end of the procession are two modern-day figures depicted to show the renewed interest and rise in popularity of the pilgrimage in the late twentieth century."

I snapped pictures of the raincoated pilgrims who gathered around the sculpture and gazed at it through the raindrops, then I turned to look at an interesting circle of 19 stones on the other side of the road with a pillar in the middle. A sign nearby explained that this was a memorial to 92 people from 19 villages in the Sierra del Perdon, the mountain pass in which the Alto del Perdon is located, who lost their lives in 1936 and 1937. It is a tribute to these victims and their families who were killed for fighting for their ideals of justice and democracy during the Spanish Civil War. They were deprived of their homes by force and buried in mass graves, forgotten, and silenced for 81 years. After taking the time to see what it represented, I thought about how few people looked over to see this meaningful memorial.

The Monument to the Pilgrims at the top of Alto del Perdon

The descent from the Alto del Perdon was steep, rocky, and very slippery, but many pilgrims hustled down the precarious decline, even as the persistent rain drizzled and covered them with a watery film, making their poles difficult to manage and their packs harder to protect. The walk from the mountaintop down to Puenta la Reina was only about 6.2 miles, but it took longer than we imagined because of the treacherous conditions. After a few hours of trekking carefully down and over slimy rocks, we were thankful when the clouds began to dissipate, the sky became clearer, and we could begin to dry off as we made our way through fields and towns.

In Uterga, we found an albergue with a restaurant called Camino Del Perdon, and we decided to stop for lunch. I got a lemon drink and a very large and delicious tuna sandwich on French bread. We found a table near the door and had just sat down when John from Seattle and his friend Mark walked in. They came over and joined us, as surprised to see us as we were to see them.

After lunch, they moved on ahead of us, and we walked the remaining miles through Muruzabal and Obanos. We passed an ancient church, Iglesia de Santa Maria de Eunate, and went through a medieval archway on our way to the next destination. Puente la Reina means "bridge of the queen" in Spanish. Located in Navarre, it is the first town after the convergence of the French Way (Camino Francés) and the Aragonese Way ("which passes from France into Spain through the more southern Somport Pass over the Pyrenees," writes Sanjiva Wijesinha in *Strangers on the Camino*). It boasts a six-arched, 11th century Romanesque bridge over the Rio Arga that was built for pilgrims on the Camino trail. The town and the bridge were named after Queen Muniadona, the wife of Navarre's King Sancho III.

Bridges can be meaningful. As we walked toward Puente la Reina, I thought about how they provide "a way across" things that are difficult. When my son and I moved to a new town, after my divorce when he was 12, he made a friend at school. Her name was Lisa. She stuck with him during the hard years, when he missed his dad who had moved farther away. I found out, after Phil died, that he'd given her my phone number "just in case." He knew his life was ebbing and that she'd keep in touch with me. She called me the day he died. She told me she knew the moment he passed away because the lights flickered and went out in her bathroom while she was taking a shower. Later, she emailed me several times to tell me stories about him I'd never heard, sometimes about things he'd done for her during the rough years of being an adolescent and a young teen.

"I was getting ready for a recital," she said. "And I was super nervous. Phil gave me a small plastic replica of Marvin the Martian, a cartoon character we both loved, and he told me to put it on the piano before I played to remind me that he was thinking about me. It helped me so much to get through that recital!"

The year after Phil died, Lisa lost a precious baby girl, who was stillborn, and she was devastated. She called me afterward to tell me about a dream she'd had that was very poignant and meaningful. She and Phil were driving together from Kansas City to Denver and, as they drove, they played music and sang along with one of their favorite James Taylor songs, "Carolina on My Mind," which happens to be where she lived now. Somewhere in Kansas, they decided to drive down a dirt road that led to an old, white farmhouse. It was deserted and they walked inside to take a look. They were surprised to find the walls covered with framed pictures and paintings. Lisa went over to look at one that caught her eye. It was of a pretty pink baby carriage sitting by itself. She knew it represented her baby, and she cried. Phil gently took it from her and said, "I'll keep it for you until you come." And she knew he meant that he would take care of her baby in heaven until she arrived. I cried when she told me that dream.

Phil was a bridge for her, even after he was gone, and she was a bridge for me, helping me meaningfully maneuver through the very painful days after his death.

At the entrance of Puenta la Reina was a large map of the town on a board next to the trail. A few pilgrims stood in front of it, plotting their course and looking for local albergues for a night's stay. We located Mayor Street and made our way down a narrow, cobbled alley lined with arches and doors that led to shops, restaurants, and hotels. We looked ahead and saw the sign for our hotel, Hotel Rural Bidean. We were surprised that it looked like little more than a second-rate restaurant, but we walked inside and waited for someone to acknowledge us.

As was often the case with small family-run inns along the Camino, one person might single-handedly check in pilgrims, while also seating and waiting on people if it also served as a restaurant. The woman behind the counter finally looked over and asked for our names. She gave us our own huge and heavy metal room keys. They reminded me of keys you might use to open a huge wooden door to a room in a medieval 13th-century castle. She pointed to a door that led to a stairway up to our rooms and indicated a small elevator inside the restaurant that could take us up to the second and third floors. We opted for the elevator, which jolted and shook when we pressed a button to take me to the second floor and Rachel to the third. When it halted abruptly on my floor, I was relieved to exit the wobbly structure, and I hopped off quickly with my luggage.

I tunneled past door after door along a very narrow passageway, looking for my room number while trying to maneuver my suitcase, and heard loud voices emerging from one door as I passed it. Somehow, I was able to navigate between the walls until I found my room. I struggled to unlock the door with the cumbersome key but finally figured out how to turn it just the right way so I could feel the lock release. The door creaked open enough for me to squeeze inside.

"Not like the Tres Reyes," I said under my breath as I looked at a small bed crammed against a wall with tiny tables on either side and a small window that looked down on a side alley. A wooden chair sat humbly in the corner between the window and the door to the bathroom. The room reminded me of Van Gogh's painting of his bedroom in Arles. I humphed and tried to be thankful as I opened the window and tried to breathe in some fresh air. As I listened to voices from the alley below that echoed up to my room, I reminded myself that I should be grateful to have made it this far. And neither my hips nor my sciatic nerve had bothered me in the least, even as I descended the challenging slope from Alto del Perdon.

"Honestly," I admitted, "they've been the least of my concerns. Thanks for that!"

Outside the hotel entrance, metal tables and chairs stood waiting for takers on Mayor Street, and a few people began to gather there to sip wine and chat. I went down and ordered wine and water with "gas" (a type of CO_2-infused, sparkling water preferred by many Europeans to "still," or regular, water), and I enjoyed sitting at one of the red-topped tables for a while before dinner. A group of men sat nearby, laughing and talking. I found out they were also walking the Camino and took their picture.

Mayor Street in Puenta la Reina

As I sat there, I glanced up to see John walking by. He and Mark had just checked into their hotels. He promised to return later with Mark and the name of a good place we could all eat dinner that evening. Rachel came down around 4, and we ordered more wine and water and sat appreciating the sunny but cool weather. We were surprised when a few small cars whizzed right past us down the narrow street, barely missing the tables, us, and groups of children and pilgrims who walked by but scooted quickly to the side as they passed. After a couple of hours, John and Mark returned to find us still sitting at the table, and we all sauntered up the street to check out two places they'd identified as possibly good. We settled on the one that was serving food earlier, but we still had to wait until 7 pm, so we walked to a contemporary gallery nearby to gaze at the art pieces displayed inside the glass walls, then we caught a wonderful view through an arch of Puenta la Reina's famous bridge.

Entrance to the bridge in Puenta la Reina

Inside the restaurant, we sat in the back at a long table and ordered from a menu. Rachel had the cod soup and told us it was good. I ordered the Pilgrim's Meal, which included wine, baked fish, fries, and Spanish flan. It wasn't as good as other meals I'd eaten, but I was thankful for the food! I sat across from Mark, who shared about his background as a lawyer for a hospital in Houston and his partner, who didn't travel as much as he did. That was why he met up with John, who also liked to travel around the world. When I realized where Mark lived, in a primarily gay part of Houston, I shared with him about my son-in-law's brother, who also lived in that area and had just lost his partner, who'd died recently.

For some reason, my heart went out to Mark. I wasn't sure why. He never shared anything intimate with me about his past or present, but I just felt a heart-burden for him.

"Lord," I prayed, "show me what I need to know."

God never revealed anything more to me about Mark's situation, but I continued to pray for him and whatever was going on in his life. My belief is that nothing happens by coincidence, and my sitting across from Mark was no exception. Often the reason for chance meetings is just that God wants us to pray for that person.

After eating, we walked back up the street and encountered a lively local band made up of townspeople who were playing a series of happy and heartwarming old songs. We clapped along as an older man conducted the motley orchestra of boys and men, who strummed and blew on instruments in a surprisingly harmonious way. As people gathered around them on the street to listen and applaud, I was impressed by the comradery that was generated and how it brought the whole town together. And I wished that my own town could pull off an event like this where so many different types and ages of people were unified, uplifted, and encouraged to play and participate together. It was the highlight of my day.

We enjoyed the music for a while then realized it was 9 pm and time for us to go our separate ways. So, we said goodbye after I took a few pictures of John, Mark, and Rachel together. I wondered if I would ever see our friends again. Such were events on the Camino. You might run into the same people many times over. Others might disappear from your life after only one encounter. One never knew what God had up His sleeve.

"Thanks, Lord, for the little blessings and inspiration You brought through these new friends and the townspeople," I whispered to myself as I walked up the steps to my "Van Gogh" room. And I wondered if my noisy neighbors in the hall or the loud voices in the alley would subside soon so I could sleep and be ready for the next day's adventure, whatever that might entail.

STEP EIGHT

ESPECIAL ESTELLA

"The instant camaraderie and welcome into the circle that is so much a part of life in this pilgrim world is lost to the fast and fear-laden society that I ordinarily live within."

—Kevin A. Codd in **To the Field of Stars**

May 13th. Saturday. Distance to Estella, 13.7 miles. At breakfast in the hotel's restaurant, we were served by a cheerless young waitress who slammed down small plates of bread, butter, jam, and jamón, and cups of coffee.

"God bless her!" I said under my breath. "She seems a bit stressed."

As I tried to chew the hard, crusty bread that I'd slathered with butter and jam to soften it up, I looked around the room and noticed a large, unusual-looking, bald man sitting by himself. He reminded me of *Doc Martin*, a character in a BBC series of the same name. I'd long enjoyed the series about a cranky doctor who leaves his job as a surgeon in the big city, because of his blood-phobia, to go to work in a small, coastal town in Cornwall, England. I wondered what this man's story was and where he was from. Was he walking on the Camino? But I didn't feel comfortable going over and asking him. So, I sat quietly chewing vigorously and sipping my coffee. Still, I couldn't help staring at him. He really stood out because of his large size and bald head with ears that stuck out. His appearance also reminded me of the character, Wallace, in Nick Park's claymation series, *Wallace and Gromit,* about an Englishman with an unusually smart dog named Gromit.

We had decided to limit our daily walks to about six or seven miles for now, until we felt more confident about walking farther. But we still had to get to our next destination, where our luggage would be waiting and our beds were reserved. I was very uneasy about not at least trying to walk the whole distance required. Wasn't that what I had trained for over the past nine months? But I felt somewhat responsible to walk together, and, at this point in the journey, I didn't feel released from any non-verbal commitment to accompany each other. I was unsure if I could make a move yet to walk at my own pace without feeling guilty. This was one mental challenge I had to figure out how overcome. What really was my responsibility? Honestly, I thought we'd agreed to walk the whole way. I hadn't anticipated or dreamed that we would need to take taxis so often. Only if it was absolutely necessary, in an emergency, I had thought. I don't think I would have agreed to taking them halfway every day! I struggled with this.

The woman at the front counter called for a cab, and we were pleasantly greeted by a put-together-looking woman who pulled up in front of the hotel and opened the doors of her van for us. She spoke some English and happily took us to Lorca, about eight miles away, driving past the Camino trail and the queen's bridge, where I could see pilgrims already walking. And I felt a heart-tug, wanting so much to join them.

We passed by many hills and avoided most of the uphill climbs, but, from Lorca, it would still be another five and a half miles to Estella. The gravel road we trekked was lined by rows of grapevines. Cypress trees pointed majestically upward in the background. I sighed at the sight and thought of our trips to Italy.

"So similar," I thought. "I would've thought I was there again."

Often the road was surrounded by mounds of red poppies that were corralled by miles of hand-built stone walls. The flowers' cheerful brightness contrasted with the dark green forests behind them and the cobalt blue, cloud-splotched skies above. They also reminded me of the poppy-punctuated pictures of Italy that hung on my walls at home.

A wooden post along the trail read *Villatuerta-Bilatorta* just before we passed under the stone arch of an ancient Roman bridge near Cirauqui, and we gasped at the surreal pastoral view on the other side. It looked like a pointillist painting!

The amazing arch-view under an ancient stone bridge

The warm sunshine bathed our faces as we sat at tables outside the Marta Café in Villatuerta. I took pictures of three adorable, dark-haired children who laughed and sang as they sat on a step across the road. Their joy touched my heart as I sat sipping my café con leche.

"So thankful for the happy innocence of children!" I sighed and thought of my grandchildren, Phil's children, who were now 12 and nine years old, around the same age as these. Every time I saw them, they reminded me of him. An expression, a glance, a word. They made me thankful, like Job, whose own children were replaced by others, and he knew, as I did, that one day he'd see them all again.

Children outside the Marta Café

As we sat there, a plump, blond woman in her 60s walked up and asked if she could sit with us.

"Sure!" we responded quickly.

Jean was originally from England but had been living with her son's family in Bermuda. Now she was walking the entire Camino Francés alone and staying at albergues along the way. It would take her more than a month, and I admired her courage and determination.

"Thanks, God, for taking care of her and watching over her," I prayed to myself.

We included her as we walked the remaining miles to Estella, crossing over a wooden bridge that spanned a clear stream, looking down at an interesting water conduit, passing by a pillar-supported cross, and resting at a fountain with a bench that commemorated the Camino pilgrims who had come this way.

Estella was built where the former village of Lizarra (Basque for "Ash" due to the abundance of ash trees around the Rio Ega) once stood. The Camino route was changed slightly in 1090 by King Sancho Ramirez, who wanted to encourage settlement in the new town. With about 14,000 inhabitants, it is a melting pot of French, Navarrese, and Jews.

"The French district was initially on the left bank," writes Leslie Gilmour in *caminoadventures.com*, "where they [the French] were granted special privileges. This lasted until Sancho the Wise allowed the local Navarrese population the same privileges and allowed them to live among the French settlers during the 12th century. Each district within the town had its own church and different groups, which led to fighting and separate hostels for pilgrims until, under Charles V, they were all merged into one."

I quickly decided, as we walked past a beautiful park along the river, then passed by the amazing arched entrance of Iglesia del Santo Sepulcro, that this was one of my favorite stops on the Camino. Another awe-inspiring cathedral, Iglesia de San Pedro de la Rúa, beckoned visitors up a series of steps that led to a massive arched doorway. I was so taken with the beautiful churches that I soon realized we had missed our turn.

I stopped a woman walking with a child and asked her if she knew how to get to our hotel on Chapitel street. She pointed us in the right direction and told us where to turn. After retracing our steps, we discovered a beautiful, arched bridge, and we gawked at the lovely panorama of historic edifices that lined the riverbanks. The sienna and rose-colored buildings sat side-by-side competing for the best overhanging balcony views of the flower-lined river.

Iglesia del Santo Sepulcro in Estella

We stopped another bystander along a narrow, cobbled street, and he pointed out our hotel. Ahead and above us, a hanging sign read *Chapitel Taberna*, and we realized that this was it, though the name on the sign didn't match our information. The location was good—on a main street close to restaurants and shops—and across the street from Iglesia de San Miguel, an ancient stone-covered monument to religious history. Assuming the name of Michael the Archangel, it was built between the 12th and 16th centuries and is another example of the Romanesque style of architecture with five apses and chapels and three Gothic naves.

We were heartily greeted by the hotel receptionist and thrilled to find beautiful, modern, clean rooms with king-sized beds and plenty of room with wonderful views of the street and the church. After unpacking and sorting through dirty clothes to take down for cleaning, I was grateful for the places that offer laundry service.

We met in the lobby around 2 pm to explore this lovely town. We walked up our street to find the town's center, Plaza de Los Fueros, where we encountered a celebration with music, vendors, and speakers. At the far end of the plaza sat Iglesia de San Juan Bautista, another beautifully-built historic reminder of the faith that has stood strong in this community over the years.

We walked around the square, peeking through doors and looking for a place that would serve us food at this hour. I was excited to find one restaurant with an A-frame display-board by the front door that showed many kinds of paella, one of my favorite Spanish dishes. We found a table inside and a pretty young woman smiled and spoke some English. She and other waitstaff answered our questions about the kinds of paella and wine they offered. I ordered a dish that was loaded with different kinds of seafood, along with a local Rioja. For dessert, I had a dish of ice cream, including vanilla, chocolate, and berry-flavored, with chocolate syrup drizzled over the top.

Estella's large and historic Plaza de Los Fueros

After eating, we made our way back to our rooms to rest and get ready for dinner. At 7 pm, we walked into the hotel dining room and were greeted by an older woman who cheerfully placed us at our reserved table. I ordered steak with fries and a salad. Soon, John and Mark wandered in and sat at a table next to us, and we caught up on the day's events. Seated on the other side of them, I was surprised to see the man I'd seen in Puenta la Reina at breakfast that morning, the one who reminded me of Doc Martin.

Across from him sat a woman I'd never seen. We said hello and I asked where he was from.

In a booming voice, he related how he'd come to walk the Camino. Hailing from Wales, David explained how he'd told his family and friends years ago that he wanted to walk on the Camino de Santiago when he retired. Like most of us, he was inspired by the movie, *The Way*. So, friends from his church banded together and, at his retirement, formally presented him with a prepaid Camino journey through Mac's Adventures. He was elated. But unfortunately, it was 2020, right when everything was shut down due to the Covid epidemic, and he had to postpone his trip. He was finally able to fulfill his dream and was enjoying every minute of walking with a goal of completing the Camino Francés in a month. And we all applauded the fact that he was able to make the trek.

But then he began to tell us scintillating stories of his hometown and how Queen Elizabeth and Prince Charles would often come through and even stay there when visiting Wales. He explained how one lady in the town was always designated as the point person for their stay, and she took her job very seriously. She would promptly contact everyone in the vicinity to give them a heads up when she knew about the Queen's arrival. The townspeople would scurry and scramble around in preparation and make sure every detail was covered and every surface was cleaned. When the Queen and the Prince arrived in their caravan of cars, the town came out to cheer and sing for them a special Welsh song. David sang it for us, and we all stopped eating to appreciate every lilting verse. Then we cheered. We were fascinated by his accent, his exuberance, and how willing he was to share the intimate details of his life.

I told David how much I enjoyed all the British TV shows I'd seen, especially *Doc Martin*, and we both commiserated the end of the last series.

"I hope they bring it back!" I exclaimed. (I recently saw that a new series started in 2024.)

We also talked about another of my favorite British series, *All Creatures Great and Small,* based on the books by James Herriot about the life and adventures of a Yorkshire veterinarian in the 1930s, 40s, and 50s. As we recalled episodes, I thought of my son, who loved to watch the older version of this series with me and then read and reread all of James Herriot's books. He even expressed a desire to go with me to England and Scotland one day to see the places mentioned in the stories. Sadly, that day never arrived.

At dinner, I was not too happy with my steak. It was so rare and tough and chewy that I couldn't eat it. After gnawing on it and not being able to swallow chunks of it, I left it on my plate and focused on my salad and fries. But I definitely enjoyed the instant comradery I felt with a new friend from Wales. As I nodded off in the large, comfortable bed in my room that night, I thought about all the unique people I was meeting on this journey.

"How wonderful and unexpected!" I thought. But just after I dozed off, my sleep was abruptly interrupted by something that wasn't so wonderful. It was the kerplop of large drops of rain splatting against my window.

"Oh my gosh," I muttered. "Here we go again!"

STEP NINE

LESSONS IN LOS ARCOS

"Perhaps travel cannot prevent bigotry, but by demonstrating that all peoples cry, laugh, eat, worry and die, it can introduce the idea that if we try and understand each other, we may even become friends."

—*Maya Angelou*

M ay 14th. Sunday. Distance to Los Arcos, 12.9 miles. I gritted my teeth when I looked out the window that morning. Yes, it was definitely still raining! Darn! After trudging down the stairs to breakfast, I was cheered up by an unexpected treat. Besides the usual hearty brown bread with butter and jam and fresh-squeezed juice and coffee, the staff was making omelets and scrambled or fried eggs with bacon to order. I opted for an omelet, but realized, after ordering bacon, that you needed to tell them "crispy." Otherwise, you were presented with the customary thin-sliced, limp, and fatty jamón.

I was pleased to see my new friend, David, with Christa, at breakfast and made sure to go over and ask for his contact information. Assuming she was his wife, I asked her for her information first. When she gave it to me, I realized she was from Germany, and they were friends who met on the trail. David went ahead and handed me a card with his information on it. Grateful, I told him that visiting Wales was on my bucket list and, whenever we could get there, we'd look him up.

"When you come," he promised, "I'll greet you with our Welsh welcoming song!" He beamed.

"I'll look forward to that!" I loved this guy! And I hoped that one day I would see him again.

John and Mark were also at breakfast, and we chatted briefly then said we hoped to see them in Los Arcos. Rachel and I met downstairs at 9:30, and the woman at the front desk called for a cab. Our plan was to have the driver take us halfway. But, as we shot through deepening puddles, the car sent water spraying from either side of us, and the raindrops grew more intense. We quickly decided to have him take us all the way to our destination, because we didn't relish the thought of walking in soggy shoes and waiting for them to dry over the next two days. But, again, I felt like I was failing in my mission to walk as much of the Camino as possible.

Los Arcos is a town of 1,117 as of 2018. It is located in Navarre, in the region of East Estella, and 38 miles from Pamplona. When we arrived there, we spotted the Adasca Café on a corner; it was open and crowded. We sloshed our way inside, avoiding the puddles as much as possible, and found a table under a temporary awning on the patio. We moved inside when a table opened up by a window. It wasn't even lunchtime, so we ordered coffee and waited until 11 o'clock to check into Hotel Monaco, which was next door to the café.

"Come back at noon," a cleaning lady in the lobby told us when we entered the hotel. "We open then."

So, we looked around for another place for coffee on the other side of the parking lot by the hotel, and we found a table inside a bakery. We ordered café con leche and sat watching an older man behind the counter as he handed fresh baguettes to customers who came in one by one. A young man with Down's Syndrome cleaned off tables and swept the floor, working around our legs and our chairs. Many local people dropped by and stared over at us, as though we were strangers from another planet who'd invaded their small space. We smiled and sipped our coffee, trying to look friendly.

At 12 o'clock, we headed back to the Hotel Monaco, climbed the steps to the second-floor registration desk and waited for the owner to come. After popping his head around the corner and seeing us standing there, he came out from the kitchen and checked us in. We discovered during our stay that this hotel was another one-man enterprise. The manager was not only the registrar, but also the waiter at breakfast in the morning. I wondered if he was also the cook.

The rain had finally stopped, so we dropped our bags off in our rooms and set out to see the town. Around a corner, we discovered the Portal de Castilla, a medieval-looking arch through which pilgrims leave the town on the way to rejoin the Camino. I wondered if the name of the town, Los Arcos (The Arch), came from this passageway. Through it, we found the large Plaza de Santa Maria surrounded by a cathedral, a café, and some lodging. Tables and chairs sat empty and waiting for pilgrims in the center of the plaza.

It was Sunday afternoon, and many of the locals were attending a mass in the Basilica de Santa Maria, which was built between the 16th and 19th centuries. I decided to go in and take a peek, and a man held one of the large wooden doors open as if to welcome me. I felt like I'd entered a page of history as I stealthily crept into a semi-dark, candle-lit, sacred space to join a mass in progress. From a back pew, my attention was drawn to the altar, which was entirely covered with gold. At the top of a massive arch, two golden angels held up a large silver crown. Beneath them, many angels hovered around a young Mary. Under that replica of the virgin, another gold-crowned Mary held Baby Jesus and sat on a throne. Below this altar stood prominent statues of the apostles, Peter and Paul.

The Plaza de Santa Maria and Portal de Castilla

Along the walls on either side of the cathedral hung crowned pulpits and a statue of the 16th century missionary, Francis Xavier, who stood on a hanging pedestal near an arched alcove, waving a cross. In the long rows of wooden benches, worshippers sat mesmerized by the priest's message as he spoke passionately from the pulpit.

To my right, a small, arched alcove gave visitors one last chance to be awed by their blessed virgin as they exited the cathedral. A gold-framed, painted mural on the wall featured Mary in scenes of visitation, with the magi below her, all in a row. I thought about how the "three kings" are held in great esteem by the Spanish people. As I sat admiring the magnificent, gilded artwork that surrounded me, I was suddenly swept up by the spontaneous singing that accompanied an organ as it rang out many choruses of "Allelujah." Surrounded by all the Mary memorabilia, I was especially moved because it was Mother's Day. And I remembered that, on this day,

44 years before, my son was born. When he died, I thought a lot about Mary and what she must have endured while watching her own dear son suffer and die right in front of her. I related to how she must have felt...the extreme helplessness and inability to do anything to save him. The pain I experienced while watching Phil suffer and struggle through every last breath was the same agony she must have born. And I felt connected to her in a much deeper way after that.

We savored as much as we could of the inspiring mass then walked quietly from the cathedral back into the plaza and down a few more streets. We watched people working outside the albergues and cafés, getting ready for the pilgrims who hadn't arrived yet, then we drifted back to our rooms.

It was 2:30, and I enjoyed gazing out my window and watching as families joined others to fill up the seats at rows of tables directly below. They embraced and shared and celebrated Mothers' Day as their children played on swings, slides, and other playground equipment behind the cathedral. Beyond the courtyard, a line of trees plumed their green leaves and white-plastered houses showed off their red-tile hats. The weather had completely cleared, leaving blue skies swept by wispy clouds that provided a beautiful backdrop for the celebrating families.

Full of rain-cleared air and small-town scenery, I rested and read until 4:30. Looking for a bite to eat, Rachel and I returned to the plaza and were surprised to find a large group of pilgrims assembling at the tables and chairs in the middle of the square. We ordered Sangria and Rioja and pizza at the café then sat with Christa from Germany at a table outside. We'd seen David at our hotel, so we communicated a message to her that he was in town. Soon joined by John and Mark, Rachel decided to go with them to the café and order a larger meal. I followed them inside and sat at a long table in a small room as they picked up their food at the café counter.

I noticed that Mark left early, and John seemed distracted and irritated. Across and down from me, he avoided looking at me and seemed more interested in talking to the people at the next table. I wondered what was

going on and almost took it to heart, but suspected that there was some
other issue I was unaware of, maybe between the two friends. I decided
not to let his churlishness bother me. I prayed for them both and that God
would heal any hurt feelings. As it turned out, this was the last time I saw
him or Mark.

The courtyard below my window in Los Arcos

As I sat at the far end of the long table, a woman came up and asked if
she could sit next to me. Her name was Sylvia. She was from Sweden, and
she was delightful and friendly. She shared her story of walking different
versions of the Camino every year. The first time she walked it with a
friend.

"But she didn't want to finish it," she said with a sigh.

And so, in the years following, she decided to walk it alone.

"It is always my gift to myself," she smiled. "I love the time alone after
serving others all year."

She was 74 years old.

Then, three women from Italy, who spoke no English, sat on the other
side of her, at the end of the table. Somehow, I was able to communicate

with them all about the places I'd enjoyed visiting in Italy. They responded with nods as if they understood. I appreciated their efforts to interpret my descriptions as we all looked at a map of Italy and pointed at places we'd been.

I sighed as I realized how much exchanging with these fellow pilgrims meant to me. Though we didn't speak the same language, we all felt a part of something bigger. And we appreciated each other for taking the time to try to build bridges that could connect our smaller worlds into one that was far more expansive. It reminded me of a prophetic quote in a devotional that I had read many months before: "You are being led out into a larger place."

"What a meaningful moment in time!" I thought as I looked around at these women who surrounded me. And I especially appreciated that we were *all* mothers far away from our homes, husbands, and children, but celebrating our lives and our journeys together on this Mothers' Day.

STEP TEN

LOVELY LOGRONO

"Some would call them Godwinks—a gentle nod from the Lord, who would send someone my way even for the briefest of times just to remind me how lucky I was. God winked at me hundreds of times on the Camino. I would often look up at the sky and wink back as a big thank-you."

—*Patrick DeVaney in* **Two Million Steps**

May 15th. Monday. Distance to Logroño, 17.2 miles. As we ate a simple breakfast in the hotel dining room, our heads swung from side to side as we watched the owner rush back and forth across the room. He hopped from one table to the next as he served us all coffee. This neck-popping entertainment was interrupted when we suddenly heard music resonating from outside the hotel. It was 7:30 in the morning! Someone went to look, and we all huddled around a window that looked out onto the parking lot. Below, a group of nine men and women made their way across the pavement, one carrying a guitar, one an accordion, another swung a lantern, and another gripped a bell. As they walked, they interrupted the morning stillness by serenading the businesses and people around us with hearty songs.

The people of Los Arcos celebrate St. Isidore's Day

"I wonder what that's all about," I said out loud.

As I walked back to my table, I spotted the man from Madrid I'd met at Hotel Akerreta.

"It's St. Isidore's Day," he explained as I walked past his table. "This day honors all farmers."

"How special," I thought. I found out later that Isidore was a Spanish saint known as a farmworker. Apparently, he worked for a wealthy landowner in Madrid, walking all afternoon behind a plow while communing with God after spending mornings in church. He loved the poor and supplied them miraculously with food. He also concerned himself with the treatment of animals. He died May 15, 1130, and was declared a saint in 1622.

"It's too bad we don't have such an honor-bestowing day in the States," I thought. So many farmers I know in the U.S. struggle to make ends meet. I wondered if it was the same in Spain. Later I read an uplifting article published online in July 2021 by *Mongabay*. It was entitled, *Spanish farmers fight forest fires with agroforestry (and many sheep)*. The article said: "During the summer, Galicia is a dry, fire-prone region of north-western Spain, which is also the continent's hardest-hit region in terms of wildfires. 2020 saw more acreage burned here than in the previous two years combined. A form of agroforestry where livestock are grazed among trees offers a solution, though: sheep and cattle graze the brush that often ignites during dry times, in an agricultural method called *silvopasture*. Not only do the trees provide food and cover for livestock, they also sequester carbon and provide habitat for wildlife while boosting farmers' incomes. Farms that implement *silvopasture* have not burned during recent fires, as one researcher tells *Mongabay*: 'Adequate management of the mountains with shepherding could be part of the solution to preventing fires.'"

The article included examples of farmers who saw the results of grazing their sheep and cattle and goats in forested areas that were not consumed by recent fires and also explained the benefits of *silvopasture* for Camino pilgrims: "30 km from Santiago de Compostela, some pilgrims on foot and others on bikes have found shade under cherry and walnut trees that comprise the *silvopasture* system of a local timber enterprise called *Bosques Naturales*."

The Camino de Santiago brings an influx of valued revenue to rural towns along the trail. And I could see why this would create even more incentive for the Spanish people to embrace their farmers who looked for ways to protect Spain's environment.

After breakfast, we taxied about 11 miles to Viana. Our eyes popped as we careened up and down winding narrow roads. More than a few times we gasped as we nearly collided with oncoming traffic. We were extremely relieved when we finally escaped from the car and the crazy driver. We walked the remaining six miles into Logroño, passing by many rows of grapevines and forested areas. One building near a park displayed a large mural that related the ongoing Camino saga with the many kinds of pilgrims who had walked or ridden this way and endured a litany of dangers along the way.

A mural along the trail

One figure on the wall rode a white horse and, coincidentally, we watched as a man camping in the park packed up to leave with his two white horses. We saw him later astride one of them. The other, loaded with bags, followed him with no lead. The man was draped in a Spanish cape and reminded me of the many ways one could traverse this trail. I admired how he honored the Camino tradition in his own way.

A man rides his horse on the Camino

Closer to Logroño, we passed by many colorful houses. One painted red had a patio facing the trail with hundreds of potted plants hung as garnishment across a black wrought-iron fence. Blue, green, yellow, and red pots completely covered the metalwork. The deck overlooking the patio was also decorated with colorful blue pots, each embracing a flowering plant.

Across from the red house, a couple greeted pilgrims with a table full of Camino mementos and drinks. I ordered a cup of coffee and my favorite lemon drink. I was thankful for their resourcefulness since we hadn't found any cafés yet along the trail.

A wonderful blend of modern and medieval, Logroño is a city of about 155,000 and is the capital of the wine-growing region of La Rioja, which gets its name from the river that runs through it, Rio Oja. Its world-famous wines trace back to the ninth century. I found Rioja to be one of my favorite red wines, and I always asked for the local version of it wherever we ate. But, according to DeVaney, Rioja wine was not always so great: "In the 1800s, an epidemic of phylloxera wiped out the Bordeaux wine region of France. Many of the French vintners brought their winemaking skills to this area of Spain, where they improved a very good product by introducing oak aging."

In John Brierley's *A Pilgrim's Guide to the Camino de Santiago*, he says: "[La Rioja is] one of the smallest and yet more diverse of the autonomous regions [regions with limited autonomy] of Spain and justifiably renowned for its superlative wines. However, it is not only its grapes that will tempt you for here you will meet a friendly people who have been welcoming pilgrims since medieval times. Indeed, kings and noblemen were promoting the camino through La Rioja as early as the XIth C as a means of exporting its famous wine and wares throughout Europe (and a way of attracting artists and stonemasons to build the great cathedrals, monasteries and monuments along the route)."

As we entered the city, we crossed a bridge that spanned the Rio Ebro, then we veered to the right to follow the Camino signs. We crossed several streets but our directions weren't very precise, and we weren't sure which way to go to find our hotel on Breton de los Herreros Street. We asked one Spanish couple for directions. Kindly responding, they took the time to converse with us in broken English; they were unsure but thought we should turn onto one of the streets ahead. We did and came across a local market with an outside display of huge trays full of amazing white asparagus, a rare find in the States.

"The unusual form of asparagus is produced by piling soil around each plant as it grows so that sunlight does not penetrate into the leaves. The lack of green chlorophyll makes for thick colourless stalks—which are delicious to eat," writes Sanjiva Wijesinha in *Strangers on the Camino*.

We crossed a side street, and were focused ahead, when a man came running over to us and pointed down the street where we stood. He spoke excitedly in Spanish and was anxious for us to look to the left. And there, a little way down, looming at the far end of the street, stood the Concatedral de Santa Maria de la Redonda de Logroño, a church with impressive twin towers. I found out later that it was built over a primitive 12th-century Romanesque temple and its name, Redonda, or "round," comes from its circular floor. The church's twin Baroque towers were built in the 18th century, and it faces the famous Plaza del Mercado, where we later found many shops and restaurants.

We finally located our hotel farther up, down the broad Breton de los Herreros street, which was lined with hotels and restaurants. It was noon when we entered the lobby of Hotel Los Bracos. It looked promising—very clean, contemporary, and impressive. But, unfortunately, the woman who checked us in was less than pleased to see us. She was irritated by our presence and questions and made it clear that our luggage had not arrived, and we were too early to get into our rooms. We figured out later, when we saw her outside smoking, that we probably interrupted her smoke-break.

A few doors down, we found a café where we ordered fried squid, a chopped salad with vinaigrette, and croquetas. We both asked for glasses of Rioja. When we returned to the hotel, our bags had been dropped off, and a friendly man at the desk was willing to hand us our keys, so we went up to our rooms. My room was smaller than the one in Pamplona, but very nice and comfortable with a double bed, desk, and clean bathroom, though I could never get my shower to work. So I took a bath.

I pulled my dirty clothes from my suitcase, shoved them into a large bag, and took them down to the front desk. We were told that someone would come to our rooms to pick up our clothes, but I waited a long time, and no one came. I grew concerned that they would not be retrieved in time to be washed and dried by the morning, so I decided to take them downstairs myself. It was 2 pm.

I rested until 4:30, when we agreed to meet in the lobby. Heading back toward the Plaza del Mercado, we found an ATM machine to retrieve more cash, took another look at the massive cathedral, then scouted around for a good restaurant that would serve us dinner before 7 or 8 pm. After peeking into several eating establishments around the plaza, we came back toward our hotel, went down a street that crossed Breton de los Herreros, and found a restaurant that was serving food. It faced a pleasant park filled with benches, flowers, vine-covered arbors, leafy trees, and 19th-century streetlamps. Perfect!

Concatedral de Santa Maria de la Redonda

First things first, we ordered Rioja and an appetizer of fried squid. These were followed by lettuce, tomato, and tuna salads topped with elegant white asparagus, sardines, and anchovies, and surrounded by quartered eggs and corn. "It doesn't get any better than this!" I thought. Before any of the food arrived, we were treated to bowls of peanuts and tasty corn nuts. As we enjoyed our salads, Rachel shared how much she missed her dogs and her home.

"I do too," I said as I thought about my dogs, Barney and Andey, a Corgi, and wondered how they were doing. I prayed a silent prayer for them. This reminded me that I was glad to be able to share our concerns as we experienced new places, people, and food. It made me think of how I appreciated having someone to walk with at times like this.

Back at the hotel, I sat in my room and felt God speaking to my heart. I'd grown much more aware of His still, small voice over the years, especially after I made early morning walks around the lake part of my daily routine almost 20 years ago. It was the one constant that kept me going through the moments when I had so many concerns about my son's life and health, and I learned how to express my pressing questions then listen for the answers. This special time always brought me a great deal of peace during highly anxious times.

"You have only walked a little this week," He spoke to my heart. "But I know you will be disappointed in yourself if you don't try to walk all the miles between Sarria to Santiago. That could be your proving ground!"

"But what about Rachel?" I asked, thinking about how hard it was for Rachel to walk between 12 and 20 miles per day because of her still-aching hips and knees. "Won't she feel deserted if I tell her I want to walk the rest of way...alone?"

"I will help you with this," He promised. "She'll understand. I'll make a way for her too, and she will learn to lean on Me more for help, just as you will."

I realized then what He wanted. His desire was that we completely trust Him along the remainder of the Camino, not just each other. It would be a new experience, and it would make a way for both of us individually to get more out of this adventure.

"Lord, You must help me to communicate this to her tomorrow so she understands," I said.

"I will," He promised.

As our conversation ended, I could hear church bells ringing outside. It was 7:30 pm.

STEP ELEVEN

SORRY SARRIA

"Life begins at the end of your comfort zone."

—*Neale Donald Walsch*

M ay 16th. Tuesday. Distance to Sarria, 326.5 miles by car. There'd be no walking the Camino today. Only driving. I dropped off my bag near the lobby at 7:30 am then headed to the dining room with Rachel. After breakfast, we went back to our rooms to wait until 10 am, when a vehicle would transport us to Sarria with a stop in León for lunch. While I read and wrote in my journal, I got a call from Tee Travel to let me know to take my suitcase with me.

When I met Rachel down in the lobby, we both retrieved our luggage from a side room. It made sense to take it with us. As we waited for what we thought would be a van with other passengers, two taxi drivers stepped into the hotel lobby. After they each read off one of our names and said we'd ride separately, Rachel asked if we could ride together. The two men went outside to discuss our request with their supervisor. They talked for a while on a cellphone then waited for a callback from him.

"What should we do?" Rachel asked me.

"Let's wait for them to tell us what's available," I said.

We'd moved outside with our suitcases, backpacks, and poles to find out if we were riding together or in separate cabs, which seemed nonsensical. Finally, after another call and much discussion, they turned to us and indicated that we should go with one of them. The first driver to show up pointed to his car. We threw our gear into his trunk then slid into the back seat for a five-hour ride with a two-hour stop.

As we talked and I edited the pictures I'd taken, I felt God nudge me.

"Now's the time to discuss the new plan," He said.

So, I broached the subject with her.

"I really feel like I'll be disappointed in myself if I don't try to walk the rest of the way," I said. "I think I can do it and at least want to try. Originally, I'd thought I could at least walk from Sarria to Santiago. We can meet up at the hotel each day."

"Ok. If you think you want to try," she said.

And that was that.

After almost three hours of looking out the windows at the changing scenery of hills, mountains, plains, woods, and towns, we arrived in León. In his book, DeVaney offers a little of the city's history: "The area was origin-inally a Roman military camp called Legio VI Victrix, or 'Victorious Sixth Legion of the Roman Empire.' The Romans spent several hundred years in Hispania, their name for the Iberian Peninsula. The town was settled here to protect the gold and silver mines and to guard the treasures moving from Las Médulas back to Rome. At the time, the Roman senate seemed more interested in Italy and the area surrounding Rome; Spain was not a popular military posting. Ruling the area was mainly a stepping-stone for politicians and generals. The best way to earn a promotion was to have an outstanding career in the army. Many Romans fought in Hispania, including General Pompey and Julius Caesar."

Our driver parked in an underground parking lot just off of Plaza San Marcelo and told us to meet him above the parking garage in two hours. We walked down a brick street called Calle Ancha and gazed into the shop windows.

"Let's go in there," I pointed to a promising jewelry shop with a sign that read *Piedras de Luz,* which is translated as "stones of light." In the window, two bright-pink plastic flamingos stood guard over just the kinds of real gem-stone rings and earrings I loved.

"Yes!" Rachel was as excited as I was. We walked into the small shop and oohed and ahhed for several minutes over shelves of beautifully-designed pieces as a very attendant shop owner pulled out drawer after drawer of jewelry to show us even more designs beyond what she had displayed.

Gemstones became more meaningful to me when I began to understand how precious and significant they are to God. When I read about how each of the 12 tribes of Israel was represented by jewels that were worn on the priest's breastplate (Exodus 28:17-29 and 39: 9-14) and how the walls of the New Jerusalem will one day be supported by precious stones that stand for the 12 apostles (Revelation 21:14,19-21), I was convinced. I also knew that when I stand before Jesus one day, He will present me with my own unique white stone with my secret name written on it (Revelation 2:17). I can't wait!

After purchasing some rings and earrings, we asked the owner if she knew of a good place to eat nearby.

"Yes!" she answered. "Right next door."

We walked back to Ezequiel Restaurant, which we'd passed by, and wondered if it was as good as the store owner had said it was. The name reminded me of a meaningful verse in the book of Ezekiel (3:8) in the Old Testament: *"I have made your forehead as hard as the hardest stone! So don't be afraid of them or fear their angry looks,"* and I thought of the beautiful gemstone rings and earrings we had just purchased and how impossible it was to break diamonds. But I also considered how the verse helped me to remember that God was there for me, even when I felt vulnerable and worried about what people thought of me or the things I'd said or done. It reminded me, when I felt like I couldn't please people or be what they wanted me to be, that it was God's approval I sought, not theirs. This was a tough lesson for me during the days and weeks surrounding my son's death, when a few people thought I should be and do things that were not possible for me. Now, this verse-reminder helped me to release any lingering worries I had about whether or not I might displease Rachel, or others, by walking the Camino at my own pace and in my own way. "Another mental obstacle checked off the list," I thought.

Our waiter at Ezequiel in León

We were seated outside at a table, where we could watch passers-by, and we were served by a wonderful waiter who brought us glasses full of good, local Rioja and water with gas. He followed these up with huge bowls of lettuce, asparagus, anchovies, tomatoes, and other vegetables. After enjoying this hearty, healthy meal, Rachel wanted to go back to the shop.

While she gazed again at the amazing assortment of jewelry and considered getting another piece, I wandered farther up Calle Ancha to Plaza Regla to take pictures of Santa Maria de Regla de León Catedral, which towers over the east side of the plaza. I was fascinated by the church's magnificent façade.

Santa Maria de Regla de León Catedral

DeVaney reveals something very interesting about the city: "Noteworthy of León is the claim that the Holy Grail is there. In 2014, a book called *Kings of the Grail* stated that after a three-year search, investigators had located the Holy Grail—the cup from which Christ drank at the Last Supper in León. It had been on display at the *Basílica of San Isidoro* since the eleventh century and had been owned by the daughter of King Fernando I. Supposedly, the king had received it as a peace offering from the Muslims. It had stood on public display—until someone announced its identity. Now, it's under lock and key."

After taking as many pictures as I could of the historic buildings on the plaza, I hurried back to join Rachel at Piedras de Luz. We walked back to the underground parking exit. While we waited for our driver to emerge,

I walked around Plaza de San Marcelo, which stands between the Old Quarter and the new León. A small garden sits in the middle of the plaza with a neo-classical fountain called the Fuente de San Marcelo, which was built in 1786, and a nearby bronze model shows the changes that have taken place in the area since Roman times. Around the plaza I could see the old town hall, or Palacio de la Paridad, Iglesia de San Marcelo, and Casa Botines, an Antoni Gaudi-designed art nouveau museum of Spanish paintings.

Our taxi came roaring up the ramp, and our driver hopped out to open the doors for us. We said goodbye to León, after our brief visit, and headed down the road to Sarria.

Sarria is a town of about 13,700 inhabitants in the province of Lugo within the autonomous community of Galicia. It serves as a popular starting point for the Camino, since the distance from here to Santiago (100 km or 62 miles) allows pilgrims to cover the necessary distance to reach the Compostela and still earn a certificate. King Alfonso IX of León died in Sarria in 1230 AD while making a pilgrimage to Santiago. In her book, *Grandma's on the Camino*, Mary O'Hara Wyman refers to Galicia as "The Land of One Million Cows" and "The Country of 1,000 Rivers."

At 5 pm we entered the town and found Hotel Alfonso IX. The unimpressive lobby looked tired and outdated, and the staff seemed overworked, which, we discovered, they were. We found our rooms up an elevator and were pleasantly surprised by how clean and modern they were. All the bathroom fixtures looked like they were made of black marble. Our beds were nice and big, and we were thankful for them. After taking showers and cleaning up, we met downstairs to walk around and ended up crossing a nearby bridge over a small waterfall to look at cafés along Rio Sarria.

After walking up and down the sidewalk, we found one place serving wine with tables and chairs outside, so we stopped there. So far, we weren't taken with the town, which seemed depressed and unkempt. After sipping our wine, we grew hungry but could find no restaurants serving food until

8 pm. Back at the hotel, we made reservations then sat outside on a covered patio drinking more wine until the allotted time.

When the restaurant doors opened promptly at 8, a herd of people suddenly appeared out of nowhere. They pushed their way inside and seated themselves at tables ahead of us. The room quickly filled up, but we were able to find a table for two in the middle of the room then waited to place our orders. One woman, the same one we saw at the front desk checking people in, ran back and forth from the kitchen, scribbling notes after taking orders from each table. She finally came to us last and took our order. And then the wait began. We found out that many of the patrons had placed their orders ahead of time so they could be served in a reasonable amount of time. Good idea, if we'd only known how bad the service was! I guess we should have suspected as much when we saw the number of staff in the hotel.

We were eventually presented with spinach croquetas and fish around 9 pm. We gulped down our food, paid our bill, and dragged ourselves up to our rooms around 9:49. I was thankful to lay down and mentally prepare myself for the next day, when I'd be walking alone for the first time. Admittedly, I felt pretty apprehensive.

"What if something happens to me along the way and my phone won't work?" I stewed. My cellphone service was nonexistent on the trails; I could only send and receive messages when I got to the hotels that offered WiFi service. How could I contact anyone if I needed help? Especially since I was walking alone, and few people spoke English....

"Ok, God," I shuddered. "This one's on You!"

Step Twelve

Pretty Portomarin

"The Camino wasn't about getting to Santiago. It wasn't about the miles we traveled. The journey was about people and the adventures we shared. It was about testing our limits, separately and together."

—*Reginald Spittle in* **Camino Sunrise**

May 17th. Wednesday. 14.9 miles to Portomarin. I stretched my arms and legs out as far as I could while lying in bed and tried to push away the anxiety I felt. I'd be walking alone today and trekking at least twice as many miles! And I thought of something my sister had texted me before I left.

"Don't walk alone!" she'd warned.

But then I thought of how many women I'd met so far who were doing that very thing...walking the Camino by themselves!

"I've never been on a journey where I feel so safe!" one woman told me. I thought of Sylvia from Sweden, who walks the Camino every year alone at age 74. And Carole from Florida, and the lady with the blistered feet on the way to Pamplona. I felt some comfort in remembering them.

I looked at my weather app and out the window. The sky looked promising, like it might be a beautiful day. It was 44 degrees, but it'd get up to about 70 degrees Fahrenheit.

"Perfect!" I thought. I'd start out wearing a fleece pullover on top of a short-sleeved shirt, and I'd bring a light jacket for later.

I met Rachel in the lobby at 7 am, and we descended the stairs to a large hall below the first floor, where people from many nationalities gathered to eat. I was surprised by how many were mulling around the cafeteria so early in the morning, and I assumed most of them were also walking on the Camino. I'd heard and read that more people joined the trail in Sarria so they could walk the minimum number of miles to earn the Compostela certificate. After eating, I hesitated then said goodbye to Rachel and went up to my room to gather my backpack and poles. I walked outside, went back over the bridge, and looked for the signs to the path. Suddenly, I found myself sighing with relief as if a weight had been lifted from me. As I followed the Camino shells and arrows along the river, I began to realize how good it felt to walk by myself in silence, with no expectation for conversation. I had not imagined how much it would mean to me to be able to contemplate my steps and my surroundings and let God lead me to whoever would walk beside me.

In her book, *Grandma's on the Camino*, Mary O'Hara Wyman says: "I am certain that my natural inclination for walking alone, and my dedication to that decision, accounted for much of my good feelings on the pilgrimage. Simply put, walking solo I was a free spirit. I didn't have to accommodate a companion pilgrim's need to push on or stop to rest or eat, to negotiate the when, where and why of each day, to talk through every decision." During my time walking alone, I grew to feel the same way.

I stepped in line behind others who moved away from the riverfront to switch back up a hill behind the buildings that lined the river. As I made my way up a narrow street that was more like an alley, I looked ahead to see a line of quaint cafés and albergues. Many pilgrims emerged from the entrances to greet the day and each other bearing backpacks and pulling themselves along with their poles. And I realized that this was the real, enchanting, older section of town, and the secret heart of Sarria we had missed. I wished we had stayed here with the other pilgrims.

At the top of the hill, I was greeted by a stone wall covered with colorful painted messages to and from pilgrims, along with a huge sign that read *Sarria*, in case I forgot where I was. When I turned to gaze back down the road I'd just climbed, I witnessed a line of smiling pilgrims moving up the hill toward me. They seemed to beam as the growing daylight reached down into the narrow passageway between the buildings to brighten their straining faces.

The impressive Iglesia Santa Marina de Sarria sat at the summit, capped by a tall bell tower and steeple. Further up a more modest church, Iglesia San Salvador de Sarria, seemed inviting with an attractive, bright-red front door topped by two smaller bells under arches. I sighed and felt blessed at the same time—I'd reached the hill's crest and was able to witness these wonderful reminders of my own and others' faith. I would never have seen any of this if I'd taken a taxi halfway this morning, and I realized how much I'd missed during the first half of the journey. This made me sad. But I was happy to be here now.

Beyond the churches was an observation deck overlooking the whole valley that embraced the town of Sarria. Knowing how much I love and appreciate good views, I walked across the road to the lookout, *Miradoiro do Cárcere*. I'm so glad I did! First, I gazed up at a time-darkened crucifix placed there on a pillar with a stone base engraved with a detailed pictorial history. Then the piéce de resistance—I breathed in slowly than exhaled as I looked out at the early morning views of the town as it woke up. Exhilarating! And I was captivated.

Miradoiro do Cárcere

Descending to the outskirts of Sarria, I looked up to see a tall bypass for cars not too far from the trail, and I crossed a narrow bridge over a scenic stream with water so clear and shallow that you could see and touch the rocks that lined the bed. I looked ahead and realized the path was surrounded by trees that leaned in toward me. And I noticed more and more pilgrims in front and behind me as I ascended a hill.

On the outskirts of Sarria

I looked out over fields of tall grass to see the bypass towering over the trees and meadows in the distance. At the crest of another hill, I realized the morning coffee was kicking in, and I had to find a restroom. This was my first experience with being a bit desperate because my need was urgent. And there was no sign of a place to stop as yet. I was getting close to a town called Vilei and found a small shop open. A middle eastern man greeted me at the door. I said "Toilette?" and he pointed to a back room then led me there. It was a tiny closet with a door that would not shut and a nasty, filthy toilet that would not flush and was filled with human waste. I had no choice but to use it. I was desperate. So, I did and quickly got out. When I returned to the front area of the shop, I noticed all the tables covered by Camino artifacts for sale. The man insisted I buy something since he'd let me use his "facilities," so I purchased a tiny shell with a ribbon and pin attached and the familiar red cross painted on it. Then I scooted out the door as fast as I could. That was my worst "stop" experience. At least I got out of there safely and relieved.

From this point on I could always find a path off the main trail where others had gone to relieve themselves or a café in close proximity. I don't know if this would have been true of the trail from Logroño to Sarria, because I didn't walk it, but from Sarria to Santiago, cafés pop up at least every hour or two along the way. It hadn't been a problem between St. Jean Pied de Port and Logroño because we walked fewer miles each day.

For the next two hours, I found the views breathtaking. I took pictures galore of stone outbuildings with pretty, potted plants alongside rustic wooden doors, homes surrounded by stone walls covered with colorful flowers, and gates garnished with lush, red-flowered vines. Stone-fenced fields overlooked valleys with views of pink-sky-topped mountains, and creeks gurgled and rippled past ferns and forests. I was particularly intrigued by a farmer who was baling hay right next to his three cows. They seemed so small under the surrounding huge and ancient oak trees.

A farmer with his cows

My next stop was a café near a town called Peruscallo. Again, needing to use the facilities after walking two hours, I headed straight toward the restroom. Seeing me going that way, a man yelled "Clientes!" And I knew he meant "customers only," so I got in line at a counter to buy some coffee. I retrieved my café con leche then headed to an empty table. I looked around as I set my cup down and propped my poles against a chair. A friendly-looking couple sat sipping their coffee next to me.

"Watch my stuff?" I pointed at my poles and coffee. I could tell they were Spanish and spoke no English, but they nodded, seeming to understand, so I high-tailed it to the restroom. When I returned, they smiled. They seemed happy to have helped me out. I was very grateful for them and thought about their kindness later as I reflected on the gnarly, gruff owner who was unwilling to oblige desperate pilgrims. It made me thankful for gracious people who sensed others' needs and willingly gave of themselves in difficult or precarious situations. I thought of Fred Rogers' famous quote about looking for the helpers whenever you faced a crisis. And I was reminded of one of the last times I went to visit my son and we walked out into his yard and sat on a bench together. Even as he struggled to breathe, he put his arm around my shoulder and hugged me close. In that one meaningful gesture, during an anxious time when I watched his health declining rapidly, he wanted to remind and reassure me of his love. Even as he struggled to survive, he was a helper.

These helpful people at the café would show up again and again along the trail, and I would have a chance to reciprocate their kindness.

A pretty potted plant at one café

Not very far from this café, I found another more charming place connected to an albergue by the side of the trail. Inside, someone had placed pretty pink flowers in a vase on top of the counter to greet customers and potted succulents in a decorative row beside the door. In the restroom, a small, square, alcoved window held a nearly-invisible green glass vase and a potted plant that captured the sunlight streaming into the room. Outside the café, tables and chairs beckoned patrons to a scenic, stone-paved patio where wood-lined islands were filled with plants.

Farther down a tree-lined path, I was passed by several families walking with their dogs. I thought of Barney and Andey at home and wished they were here walking with me. "They would love this trail!" I sighed and imagined them sniffing at the strange plants and people all around them. In the months of preparation for the Camino, I had often taken them with me to walk on a wooded trail near my house. They had loved the sights and sounds of the forest: the deer, squirrels, black-capped chickadees, egrets, blue jays, tiger swallowtails, red-bellied woodpeckers, tufted titmouses, buzzards, cardinals, and many beautiful wildflowers. And they loved to inspect it all!

As I watched the families pass me on the path, they reminded me of Phil's desire to have his own family. He especially wanted this after my divorce and his sister went off to college, and he felt like we were all alone and fending for ourselves. I remember when he first introduced me to his fiancée, after he moved to Denver, and how elated he was and proud that he'd found someone to spend the rest of his life with. He'd been honest with her about his lung disease, but they both hoped for the best in the years they would have together. After they were blessed with twin boys and a sweet baby girl, he was only able to enjoy this dream-come-true for a short time, but he treasured every moment with his children before he died. He would pull out his guitar and sing to the boys while he could. And they would sit at his feet and gaze up at his fingers as they moved magically over the strings. My heart broke when I saw the look of angst in his eyes when he could no longer sing. He realized then that he'd only have a brief time to appreciate this family he had helped to birth. It was hard for me to watch as his dream came to a close. But I also knew he would spend eternity with them one day and this gave me great hope.

I came across a small stone church with wooden doors under an arched doorway topped by the same bell-gable, called an *espadaña,* as the churches I'd seen in Sarria. A stone baptismal font sat in front and reminded me of rebirth. Behind the church, rows of cross-topped mausoleums held enclosed vaults with inscriptions and flowers. These made me and other passers-by think of death and the hereafter.

As I walked among the vaulted walls, I watched as pilgrims paused to gaze in hushed silence. After admiring how the dead were honored here, I saw beautiful red roses blooming beside the cemetery, probably planted in someone's memory. Not too far from away, I found a stone bench with an arched stone-back set against a tree beside the path. I felt like it was placed here as a reminder of life and our need to take time to rest and reflect.

I passed by a large group of Asian pilgrims who'd stopped to rest beside a café. Many wearing straw and bamboo "coolie" hats, they sat under trees and congregated near the building. This was not the last time I saw them. They weren't hard to miss, since they were the only large group of people traveling together. I wondered what it was like to experience this pilgrimage with so many others. If I were to travel this way, would I lose out on the moments I was growing to embrace? Would I still be able to reflect and contemplate and breathe in all the sights and sounds without feeling obligated to converse or compromise the silence?

Close to noon I began looking for a lunch stop and was intrigued by a place where a tiny Spanish woman, maybe four feet tall, greeted people at the entrance of a garden enclosure with a sign that indicated everything inside was "donation only." I ventured in and found a counter loaded with food and drinks for the taking. A casserole dish full of a savory noodle and meat mixture sat invitingly. I helped myself.

"How wonderful!" I thought. "Such a generous heart."

A table beyond the counter beckoned to me, and I was immediately touched to see a colorful patio next to me, where pilgrims sat surrounded by pots of plants and flowers: orange, purple, blue, pink, and red. On the other side of the patio was an enclosed area filled with potted plants and flowers and a wheelbarrow full of red, blue, and pink flowers. It was like a miniature Garden of Eden. "Very inspiring," I thought. The whole place made me smile. I could see that it affected others in a cheerful way too as I looked around. Many pilgrims sat resting in chairs as they enjoyed the tasty food and refreshing drinks from her buffet.

I tipped the woman generously when I left. But, before I moved on, I ran into the Spanish couple who'd watched my stuff at the café. I tried to converse with the husband while he stood outside the restroom and waited for his wife to emerge. He was able to communicate that they were from Barcelona. When the wife came out, he beckoned for me to go on in. I acknowledged them both, and they returned my smile. Soon afterward, I saw the husband sitting on a rock ledge, grimacing. He held his bare foot in one hand, and I could tell he had a painful blister. I walked over and pointed to his foot.

"Do you need something for your blisters?" I asked.

He seemed to understand and pointed to his wife who was rummaging through her backpack. Though I spoke no Spanish, I understood his response: "She has something."

I nodded, smiled, and turned back to the path. I loved this couple who tried so hard to communicate with me, even though they had no idea who I was or where I was from.

Hiking boot "planters" along the way

After my lunch stop, I saw many more ancient stone buildings. On the side of one, a vine loaded with gorgeous red flowers exploded in full bloom. Another was decorated with rows of wooden racks that were covered with Camino shells for sale. A pair of hiking boots used as a planter for succulents sat atop one stone wall. I often saw discarded boots used this way, and I wondered if they were left behind by hikers who were tired of the blisters they caused, or if the boots had just worn out around their feet. Hopefully they had another pair of shoes to wear.

At another stop near a town called Vilachi, I couldn't resist another refreshing limón drink. It picked me up as I walked the last long leg of the journey. I looked ahead and was mesmerized by a farmer herding five cows up the road toward me. A watchful dog ambled along beside them, making sure they didn't veer from the road. The animals strolled slowly past me, not at all concerned about my presence, even though I was within a few feet of them. They eyed me gently, and I smiled at the feeling of peace they gave me.

A farmer herds his cows down a road by the trail

Farther along, a leaning cross held many small stone reminders on its outstretched arms and hovered beside a Camino marker, and a dog lay in the grass near the path looking back toward the herd of sheep he was guarding. I never saw any dogs on leashes while walking along the trails.

The farther I went, the more energized I felt. I smiled and said, "Buen Camino" to every person I passed by, and each one responded in a friendly manner. I was so grateful that I could walk the miles without feeling tired. I was also thankful to this point for my Hokas, which were consistently comfortable and never rubbed my feet. But now, as I walked many more miles, I noticed that the edges of my big toes were feeling raw and starting to hurt. I could feel blisters forming.

Around a bend I watched two pilgrims make their way down a hill. Ahead of them, a body of blue water colored the valley and was surrounded by hills filled with green trees. A rock ledge wound down along the edge of the road, and, beyond the reservoir, I could see a town planted and waiting among the hills.

"Must be Portomarin," I thought hopefully. And my heart grew lighter as I drew closer.

The final descent to Portomarin

Nearer the destination, I noticed two possible ways to proceed. More people headed in one direction, so I chose this path. But I quickly realized that this seemingly shorter way held a hidden hazard: a very steep and rocky decline. I stood over it and looked down at the precarious passageway.

Then I noticed a middle-aged woman and two younger women making their way down. The two young ones at the bottom were helping the older one by holding her poles as she descended. As I watched, I made an executive decision. Gripping my poles for so many miles had caused my hands and fingers to grow very stiff and sore. One thumb was growing rigid from accelerating arthritis. I also felt like it would be next to impossible to maneuver this steep decline while holding onto them. As I gingerly began to make my way down from the top, I yelled over to the women.

"Would any of you like my poles?"

"I can hold them for you," one of the young women called back.

"No, you can have them if you want them!" I shouted.

"Really? Are you sure?" she yelled, her eyes wide.

"Yes! Please take them!"

I climbed down as far as I could, holding the poles out to her as she reached up to grab them. When she took them from me, I suddenly felt free in a way I hadn't expected. It was like a load had been lifted off of me. I hadn't realized how cumbersome trying to navigate with the poles had been. And I thought back to all the times I'd had to stop and unwrap the strap from around one hand and move that pole to the other hand so I could reach into my pocket and get my phone out to take a picture. Now I wouldn't have to worry about making my way down slopes filled with rocks where I could slip and fall with my hands tied to the poles. Hallelujah! Now I was free of them! I felt liberated.

After groping my way successfully down the hill, stone by precarious stone, and finally reaching the level path below, I sighed with relief. I passed the three women and saw the older woman helping the younger one who'd taken the poles. She was adjusting them for her and showing her how to use them. They all turned and smiled.

"Perfect!" they said and nodded toward the poles. I realized at that moment that this gift was meant to be. It was a token of kindness that blessed me and those I'd reached out to.

Soon, I came to a long bridge that crossed the beautiful blue Belasar reservoir. Close to the entrance, Asian pilgrims stood together near a platform snapping pictures of the spanning bridge. In front of them, a heart-shaped stone monument held a bell with an inscription that read *Liberty Bell.* I discovered that it signified the freedom and unity of the people of this area, and I wondered about the reason and need for the reminder.

The Fichier Bridge into Portomarin

About a century ago, a small village sat near the current location of Portomarin on the Rio Mino with an old Roman bridge that crossed the river. In the 1960s, the government decided to dam the river and create a reservoir. As a result, the old village was flooded out. They were able to save some of the historical buildings beforehand by moving parts of the town to a new location above the reservoir. This included the Igrexa de San Xoán, one of Galicia's historical Roman structures, which now sits in Portomarin. But their attempts to save some of the old village's history never adequately addressed the resultant feeling of rootlessness among those who chose to stay in the new town.

According to an online article in *Nature Journal* called *Emotional conflict and trauma: the recovery of stolen memory using a mixed-methods approach,* many of Portomarin's inhabitants wondered how they could save their inherent identity and pass it on to future generations? How could education about the past help them overcome their feelings of being cut off from their roots? They encouraged the schools to foster a dialogue about what had transpired, and this helped everyone overcome the trauma. From this, they were able to construct a shared identity between the younger and older inhabitants. I am pretty sure this heart-shaped monument was a result of these efforts.

I enjoyed looking out over the reservoir as I walked across the pedestrian pathway that spanned the long bridge, high above the water. I watched the pilgrims ahead of me and looked up at the town that hovered above us on the other side. I could see boats below and, in the distance, large homes that stood on the hills between the shore and groups of trees. Along some hillsides, planted terraces stepped down toward the water, while tile-roofed buildings stair-stepped back up the hills toward the woods.

On the other side of the bridge, stairs built with stones from the old village made their way up a steep hill. At the top stood an archway, also made with stones. I walked through it and found a large metal sign that said: "*Portomarin...estrela dos desexos.*" *Estrela dos desexos* means *star of desire*, implying that Portomarin was one of the stars pilgrims would encounter while pursuing Compostela, *the field of stars.*

The entrance into Portomarin

The directions to the hotel said to turn right after the bridge, so I did. I walked up Rua do Peregrino past a park with views of the reservoir and saw a family enjoying a picnic at a table. I reached the end of the road with no sign of the hotel. So, I walked to an albergue across from the park, went inside, and asked a woman who greeted me if she knew where I could find Hotel Ferramenteiro. She walked outside with me and pointed back down the road toward the entrance and the steps.

"On the other side of the bridge, on Camino da Capela street," she said.

"And a pharmacy?" I asked, thinking of my aching big toes and the blisters forming on them.

"Go to the end of this road, the way you were headed, then turn left, then go left again onto the next street, Rua do Mino," she said.

I opted to go to the pharmacy first, so I headed in the direction she indicated. I found Rua do Mino lined with colonnaded entrances to cafés and hotels. Many people sat outside drinking wine and beer since it was around 3 pm. I looked at their faces, wondering if I might spot Rachel, feeling sure she was already here.

I walked past white-washed buildings with hued-stone arches and attractive stone-framed windows with balconies that hovered over the car-lined street. I saw no sign of a pharmacy, so I stopped a friendly-looking waitress carrying a tray of drinks. She pointed up the street. So, I kept walking. When I finally spotted a blue cross, the sign for a drug store, I also noticed the *closed* sign in front. Often their hours were Monday to Friday from 9:30 am to 2 pm and 5 pm to 9:30 pm. I would need to return later. Exhausted, I kept walking almost to the end of Rua do Mino, then crossed Rua do Peregrino onto another street, Camino da Capela. Winding to the right, I finally saw the hotel and let out a sigh of relief. It was 3:20 and my feet throbbed, especially my big toes.

When I trudged through the front door of the hotel, I was relieved to see my suitcase sitting there waiting for me patiently by the receptionist's counter. A friendly face greeted me, and I was immediately drawn in by the glowing cheerfulness of the place. Perched up on a hill that overlooked the reservoir, the lobby embraced a beckoning view through large windows that opened onto a covered deck where guests were entranced by the sparkling blue water. It all gave me the feeling of being at a vacation resort. The whole town seemed to give off this vibe. Everyone I saw looked and acted like they were "on holiday" and appeared very happy to be here.

I quickly found my room on the first floor and was thankful to have two neatly-made twin beds decorated with bright red pillows. The walls of the spacious room were lined with panels of red and gray and, above the beds, artistic renditions of reddish-purple flowers beckoned to me to lay down and rest a while. I texted Rachel to let her know I'd made it, then I took out all my dirty clothes to wash. It was sunny outside and I wanted to take advantage of my own private deck with a table and chairs and a remarkable view of the reservoir. After washing some things, I draped them over the outdoor furniture to dry. Then I showered and ministered to my aching big toes. I cleaned the blisters, applied healing antiseptic salve to them, then covered them with moleskin patches. I would let my feet air out by wearing thongs for a while.

The deck off my room

Rachel and I met in the lobby at 5:30, ordered glasses of Rioja at the front desk, and sat outside on the deck. It was a beautiful, sunny evening. A man and his son came out to join us, and we started a conversation. The father, from Pennsylvania, told us how he and his son had wanted to do the Camino together for years and were finally able to make the journey together. The son, Christopher, lived in Ohio and studied psychology at a local college but wanted to somehow incorporate spirituality into his curricula. He was Catholic and had thought about going into the ministry but decided to move into a more secular track. But he still wanted his beliefs as part of his pursuits. I thought of a book I wanted to recommend to him: *Chasing Francis* by Ian Morgan Cron, about a young man who questions his faith but then rediscovers his beliefs and affirms his calling when he goes to stay with a related monk in Assisi, Italy.

Christopher's search reminded me of my own son as an adolescent and young teen. He also sought to discover his identity and calling as his faith grew. But, after I divorced, and we moved, he groped to find his way. One day, as we tried to arrange the furniture in his bedroom in our duplex, he became very emotional as he confessed something to me.

"Mom, I want to go back to fellowship."

We had stopped attending the home-based Bible study group we'd been a part of for many years, before his dad and I had separated.

"I miss how we used to get together with the other believers." He looked like he might cry. And I knew he missed the people who gathered in our living room to sing songs, play guitars, and share meaningful verses. He loved them, and they always included him in every part of our get-togethers.

Because of his request, I found a group who met nearby, and we started attending Bible fellowships together. That reconnection changed his life...and mine. It was his longing for meaning that opened the door for me to find my way back onto my own faith path.

We ran into Christopher and his dad again when we went up the street to O Mirador for dinner. They were seated at a table near ours, and we waved at them on the way out. Inside the restaurant, I was surprised to see life-sized plaster renditions of Elvis and a cowboy with a leather strap full of bullets around his neck and a lasso under his arm.

"How funny to see these here," I thought.

Statues in the restaurant, O Mirador, in Portomarin

We sat on a deck with a view of buildings, palm trees, and the reservoir, and we watched as pilgrims arrived and greeted each other on the street below. We enjoyed salads with fresh lettuce, avocadoes, tomatoes, cucumbers, and smoked salmon sprinkled with pumpkin and sesame seeds, and, of course, regional red wine. We had also come to love the Spanish flan for dessert, especially the coffee flavored.

It felt good to sit, rest my sore feet, and savor a delicious meal. I stepped tenderly back to the hotel, only two doors down, thankful I had a comfortable bed to sleep on. I had clocked in close to 18 miles. How many would I be able to walk tomorrow? I cringed as I looked at my raw, blistered toes. But thought hopefully of the people I'd met so far and wondered who I might meet next and what surprises they would hold for me to discover.

STEP THIRTEEN

REVELATIONS ON THE WAY TO PALAS DE REI

"I am learning something here about the camino: an expansive generosity and spontaneous kindness has been woven into this way that begins to touch us all, making us more caring ourselves and then more trusting. Step by step we are walking out of our fear. We are learning that it is easier to care than to not care. We are being softened even as our feet are being toughened."

—Kevin A. Codd in **To the Field of Stars**

May 18th. Thursday. 14.9 miles to Palas de Rei. At 7 am, we found a table next to the lobby's large windows and went to help ourselves to the usual breakfast fare. I was surprised and delighted to discover one wonderful addition. A *Tarta de Santiago* sat unassumingly on the long counter amidst all the other food. This famous Spanish almond cake to honor pilgrims on the Camino was referred to as far back as 1577. Legend has it that a pilgrim brought it to Galicia and shared it with others on the journey to Santiago. Simply made of eggs, almonds, and sugar, its uniqueness comes in the form of the bright red cross of St. James emblazoned on top to thrust through its pilgrim message of sacrifice. Of course, I had to have a slice. It was chewy and delicious, though a little on the dry side. But I appreciated the effort made to offer it and its underlying meaning.

After eating, I went to my room, gathered up my backpack, and headed out the front door. I didn't see Rachel on the way out, but I felt less apprehensive this time about walking alone. Through the lobby windows, I'd seen other pilgrims making their way toward a bridge down the street behind the hotel. So I followed several of them to the road below and crossed a footbridge over Rio Torres. I gasped when I saw the view.

The bridge into Portomarin walked across the water in the distance, surrounded by a wispy fog that drifted up dreamily toward a cobalt-blue, cloud-filled sky. In the foreground, puffs of mist danced across the water toward me then dissipated a few feet from the shore that wound around in front of me. Three boats, attached securely to a small dock, bobbed precariously as the mist danced around them. On the far shore, a white house sat perched on the shore as white smoke plumed up into the air.

"What a magnificent sight!" I whispered.

The view from Portomarin across the reservoir

After absorbing as much as I could of the amazing haze-brushed "painting," I turned to face my path. Pilgrims were moving away from the road and up the steep Mount San Antonio, disappearing into the trees. I appreciated their silence as I huffed and puffed behind them. And I was thankful I had the strength to get to the top, where I was rewarded with sun-spattered splashes of little yellow flowers that popped up beside the path. Several stone-faced, quaint, and ancient buildings graced the scene as the number of pilgrims joining the trail grew by the hour.

I especially noticed one man with a bandaged knee, and I was touched by his persistence to walk despite his apparent pain. I saw quite a few people on the trail like this—individuals burdened by physical ailments but still pursuing the path. I wondered if some wanted to gain healing along the way.

An injured pilgrim on the trail

One of my unexpected and delightful finds along the way was the fragrant and enchanting eucalyptus forests. Apparently, these weren't always a part of the Spanish landscape. They were introduced to Galicia in the 19th century when a monk brought some seeds from Australia, where he'd been a missionary. They adapted well and spread rapidly throughout the region. As I walked along a dirt road, I'd suddenly find myself engulfed in a magical and surreal wooded area where the trees reached up and eclipsed the sky and the ground beside me was covered with springing beds full of green ferns and lined by stone walls covered with moss. If there were leprechauns, surely they would live in this place!

Pilgrims walking among the trees

People would stop and remove their backpacks just to rest, breathe in the wonderful fragrance, and take in the shady scented scene.

Beyond the woods, I found a café near Gonzar called El Descanso del Peregrino and stopped for coffee. As I stepped in line to order, I was surprised to find myself standing next to the three women I'd met going downhill on the way to Portomarin. One of them was still holding my poles. I excitedly haled them and took their picture. They were happy to see me too. Café con leche in hand, I stepped around many tables looking for a place to sit. All seats were taken, so I headed to an area behind the café. And there they were!

"Come and sit with us!" the three invited.

So, I pulled up a chair, threw off my backpack, and plopped down beside them. A mother traveling with her two daughters, Kathy was retired from the Canadian postal system. Shawna, who took the poles, was the talkative one. Her job in Canada was to work for a nonprofit company that serviced the elderly. Tanya lived in England and worked for a business in London.

We chatted a while, finished our coffee, then walked together to the next stop, Castromaior.

Three women from Canada

Along the way, Shawna asked me questions about my job as a financial advisor, and I shared about how I'd recently transitioned my business to three women in my area. And I thought about how God had led me to wonderful and talented people to whom I could confidently transfer my clients. I had spent the last 25 years developing relationships with many amazing individuals with whom I shared confidences, life events, and meaningful memories. It was hard to let them go, but I knew the time had come. I just had to find the right people with the needed skillsets to best serve them. God led me in miraculous ways to some very gifted women and, in the end, I felt comfortable handing off my clients to each of them. I was thankful as I looked back on how smoothly the process had gone.

Shawna and I touched on other topics like planning for retirement, and she mentioned a firm she and her husband had been working with. She trusted the advisor they met with, she said, and he had done a good job for them.

"That's all that matters," I reflected.

The three women decided to stop for lunch at another café. I wasn't hungry, so I bid them farewell, used the restroom, and went ahead. It made me feel good that I could see Shawna appreciating the poles as we walked.

I passed several carved wooden creatures near the trail: a bug-eyed giraffe stood next to a pig and an elephant, while a huge gorilla hovered over them both. They all guarded a metal container inside the notch of a tin-roofed tree stump.

Carved wooden creatures along the trail

Layers of red poppies brightened a stone wall in one neighborhood and brought me a little "pick me up" and late-morning cheer, and a large white cross on a stepped platform reminded me to turn my thoughts in God's direction.

I stopped at a café called O Cruceiro to eat a croissant with cheese and a banana I'd brought from breakfast that morning. I turned to see Christopher, the young man from the deck at the hotel in Portomarin, and I walked over to tell him about the book I thought he might like called *Chasing Francis*. He asked for my name. Then I asked if he knew what his own name meant.

"Christ bearer," I said. "You know God's hand was on you."

"Yes," he nodded. "And His hand is on you too!"

My son, Phil, was a "Christ-bearer." He spread a message of deliverance to many who crossed his path. While he lived in Littleton, Colorado, the Columbine High School shooting took place. It was April 1999, and many people in the area were inconsolable. He and a friend grabbed their guitars and plopped themselves down in the middle of a park across the street from the school. And they sat for hours, strumming, singing, and talking to anyone who passed by. There's no telling how many young people were reached that day, and in the days that followed, through a musical message of hope and peace.

Still pondering this memory, I passed by an impressive cross, where several people gathered to pray. Next to a gnarled oak tree, a 17th century cross stood on a pillar that rose from four stone steps. If you faced the front of it, you could see Jesus on a cross with a Camino shell beside him. I was moved to see so many memorial stones and notes at its base, and I thought of how many roadside prayer requests I'd seen.

Another historic cross on the trail

Farther on, a beautiful burst of large red flowers leaned over to greet me. They bent down as they bobbed on their stems, almost completely covering the metal that crowned the top of a wall. As I stood gazing at the scenic beauty that seemed to spring from every corner, a young woman suddenly stepped forward. She pointed toward a small, humble, stone building beside the trail and invited me to follow her inside.

"Restroom?" I asked, thinking of my current need and not knowing if she spoke fluent English.

"Yes, yes!" She beckoned for me to follow her inside then pointed to a door in a room beyond the entry. When I came out, I noticed a table that held a wooden cross, a lantern with a candle, a small basket, two shells, hand sanitizer, Dutch clogs, a small sign that read "Relax," a wooden box with red and black berries inside, and a large sign above the table that said, "Bienvenidos! Welcome! La Fuente del Peregrino, Ligonde km 75, 1999." Another table in the small room held a journal where pilgrims could write messages, a cup of pens, two shells, and another lantern with a candle. Above the table was a pictorial sign that said "Buen Camino" and told the story of the donation-only albergue that is a part of this building.

The pilgrim refuge at La Fuente del Peregrino

I wandered back out to the front room, and another young woman approached and asked me to place a pin near my home city. On a large world wall map covered with colored pins, I saw that someone had placed a pin into Kansas City. I wondered if Rachel was here earlier.

"Where are you from?" I asked, and she explained that she and another young woman behind a table full of Camino trinkets were students from Cairn University in Pennsylvania. They'd volunteered their summer to work along the Camino so they could help passing pilgrims. I believe they also wanted to bring others a message of hope. We talked for a while, and I was impressed by their commitment and desire to serve. I took their picture and thanked them for their hospitality.

I asked what they hoped to achieve down the road. One expressed her desire to work in finances, so I told her about my background as a financial advisor and how much I enjoyed it. I recommended that she investigate any opportunities to work with my company by approaching offices near her home. I hoped my words encouraged her.

The young women volunteers at La Fuente del Peregrino

I thought of my aspirations when I was 19 and 20 years old. How much I wanted to combine my belief in God with a ministry pursuit of some kind! As a teen, I thought about joining the Peace Corps or VISTA (Volunteers in Service to America). But the idea never dawned as other opportunities seemed to shine brighter. I quit college my sophomore year to get married, have kids, and focus on full-time ministry. My husband and I were deeply involved with an organization that offered us training on how to start and lead classes and local home-based Bible-study fellowships. Moving often when asked, we birthed new groups, taught, and led others to understand the Bible. But, as the years sped by, instability from alcoholism persisted and abuse increased to undermine and threaten the foundations of every effort we undertook. My dreams seemed to fade from view. I was crushed and unsure of how I could ever achieve my youthful aspirations.

As my marriage fell apart, I returned to college, got a degree in business communications and went to work for an insurance company. I ended up as a financial advisor through a circuitous route that only God could have mapped out. And my job allowed me the opportunity to minister to many people, not just by helping them with their financial situations, but by offering counsel in other areas of their lives—mental, familial, physical, and spiritual. I reflected on how I'd somehow been able to achieve my long-sought pursuit. It seemed all so crazy to me now.

"It is possible," I said to the young women. "You can reach whatever dream you have with God's help. And often it comes about in ways you never expected!" I smiled knowingly.

I asked if I could pray for them. Without hesitation, they gathered around me, and we stood in a circle in the middle of that tiny room in the humble, historical, time-worn building. I prayed for their journey and for God's hand to be on them and their pursuits. Then I thanked them for their service. I left that memorable moment feeling very blessed by this divine appointment.

As I walked away, I recalled the overwhelming struggle I'd faced in my mid to late 30s. I had to finish college, apply for a divorce, and find a job...all within six months! I sighed as I reflected on this time that was so very painful, not just for me, but for Phil. He lost all his friends, his wonderful neighborhood where he enjoyed skateboarding, and the dad he cared about, when we had to move because of my new job. It was difficult, I reflected, but not nearly as traumatic as the days that led up to his death. Divorce is dreadful, but it can't compare to losing a child one adores.

Back on the trail, the path ran downhill over rocks beside a spring. It was a little hard to manage as I descended the steep decline, but it leveled out after a while, and I passed a farm where a small dog lay contentedly sunning himself in front of the door of an out-building. I thought again about Barney and Andey and how much I missed them. A carved statue of St. James on a huge tree stump with a blue cross hanging around his neck reminded me to pay attention to my current pursuit. And a yellow painted arrow pointed to the right, where an historic stone church stood surrounded by a stone wall. I ended up in another graveyard with rows of vaults filled with flowers and topped by crosses.

The vaulted tombs in a graveyard

My feet were sore, and I was relieved to spot a sign for Palas de Rei, a town of about 3,000 people. I wondered about the town's name and what it meant, so I looked it up. "The name Palas de Rei is supposed to come from Pallatium regis (royal palace) because it was the residence of the Visigothic monarch Witiza at the beginning of the 8th century," says *vivecamino.com*. "The history of this quiet village is...closely linked to the French Pilgrim's Way to Santiago de Compostela. The *Codex Calixtinus* [the first account of the pilgrimage written in the 12th century for Pope Calixtus II by French scholar Aymeric Picaud] records that the final stage to the tomb of the apostle starts from this point, 68 kilometres [42.25 miles] of a journey that...Picaud defined as 'moderate.' Thus, with the medieval boom in pilgrimages, the locality underwent a significant expansion. The town of Palas de Rei...was one of the favourite places of residence of the Galician nobility."

I turned off the trail too soon and found myself in a busy part of town with no sign of the street I was looking for, Rua do Mercado. I walked farther and farther down a main street and decided to stop a Spanish couple to ask for directions. The man spoke a little English, and he tried very hard to help me by looking at his phone, but he couldn't find the street either. He suggested continuing up this street toward the center of town. I did and, though the roads weren't marked well, I had a hunch to turn down one to my left. Still not seeing any sign of the hotel, I stopped at a bar. Feeling a little intimidated, I stepped inside to face a room full of gruff-looking men who all stopped talking and stared at me, their eyes drilling through me.

"Does anyone speak English?" I asked bravely, hoping to be able to communicate with at least one of them.

No one spoke up.

"Casa Benilde?" I offered.

A man rattled off something in Spanish and pointed in one direction. But another man argued with him then walked outside. Beckoning to me, he steered me around a corner and pointed up a street.

"Ok!" I nodded and thanked him and sighed.

I was exhilarated to discover a door with a sign next to it not too far down the street. *Casa Benilde,* it announced. Inside, I was greeted by a very friendly and cheerful woman who spoke fluent English. Professional and eager to help, she checked me in, stamped my Camino passport, then called a woman to take me up to my room. She also explained where to go for breakfast. I was impressed by this expertly-run, beautiful, and historic hotel in the middle of the town, especially after traipsing past many worn-looking, deteriorating, and uninviting buildings on my way here. My room on the third floor was small and had a single bed, wardrobe, and a private bath. But it boasted a wonderful view of a garden surrounded by trees and ancient stone buildings with tiled roofs. It was 3:20 pm and I texted Rachel that I was here. Then I washed clothes, showered, rested, and ministered to my throbbing, blistered toes.

We met downstairs at 6 pm, walked to a pharmacy where I bought tape to wind around the hiking wool for my toes. She'd made reservations at Restaurante Folgueira for 7 pm, so we headed that way. We were seated in the back at a corner table and watched as many other pilgrims streamed in. We ordered a rice and lobster dish to share, with salads, bread, and Rioja. We really liked our waiter, a heavy-set, balding man with a dent in his forehead. He reminded me a little of a cartoon character, but was friendly and tried his best to provide us with good service.

Our waiter at Restaurante Folgueira

We were grateful for a good meal and even more thankful to "hit the hay" at 8:30. I lay in bed, wondering what the next day would bring and who I'd meet the next day. Life on the Camino was so unpredictable. But it was exciting to me and held so much mysterious adventure. I loved it! Especially the "God-winks" and divine encounters along the way. I thought about the young women I'd met at La Fuente del Peregrino. And I almost didn't want it to end. But I realized that I had only two more stops before arriving in Santiago!

STEP FOURTEEN

ARDUOUS ARZUA

"One thing I notice out here is that everyone is equal: language, nationalities, and cultural differences seem to disappear or at least recede in importance as we all go through the same experience day after day. Everybody is in this together yet everyone is really doing it alone and is experiencing it alone. It has its effect on us, I think. The camino is doing something to us internally but we don't know exactly what—we sense it—but can't put our finger on it yet."

—*Kevin A. Codd in* **To the Field of Stars**

May 19th. Friday. 17.4 miles to Arzua. After rising at 5:30 to read and pray, I met Rachel outside my door at 7:30, and we walked down to a basement level room to be greeted by a man wearing a white coat who asked if we wanted coffee. As I turned to find an empty table, I was amazed to see the Spanish couple I kept running into along the trail.

They were seated at a table for two against a wall. I went over excitedly, and they greeted me in Spanish. I could tell they were as glad to see me as I was to see them. And surprised.

My Spanish friends

After trying to converse with my new friends and wolfing down my breakfast, I was on my way by 8:15. I walked down a street behind Casa Benilde and followed other pilgrims past an open market, where two people haggled over a cage of rabbits. I took pictures of a beautiful fountain honoring St. James on the way out of town and a more modern statue that depicted pilgrims waving their arms in the air as if in praise. Another simple memorial created by passing pilgrims caught my eye. Hundreds of stones representing prayers were placed on two cement blocks. How many of these reminders had I seen now on the Camino? Farther down, I came to a trench-like gully surrounded by a dense canopied forest. Cliff-like embankments stood on either side, and I felt like I was trudging through a tunnel. I passed several horreos—small huts built of wood or stone and raised from the ground by pillars or stone and cement pedestals. Found in northwestern Spain and northern Portugal, these are used to store grain and other things to protect them from rodents.

I ran into my Spanish friends two more times that day, once by a café restroom, where they sat on a ledge resting and waved. Again, next to a pasture filled with cows, they stopped to take my picture.

I continued to O Coto and came across a very interesting hotel called Casa de Los Somoza, which was a white-plastered building with exposed brown stones. It was surrounded by fascinating statues, including a life-sized one of St. James. A group of pilgrims lined up for pictures with the saint.

Statue of St. James near Casa de Los Somoza

Beside the hotel, a beautifully-landscaped area beckoned to passers-by with statues that represented the local culture. I took a picture of two that depicted a man playing bagpipes and a woman in local historical dress tapping on a tambourine. Beds of red roses decorated the area around them.

I continued through woods and over a bridge and came upon a small community called Leboreiro. An unusual, thatched-roofed horreo on top of a cement pillar caught my eye, and I took a picture of it.

Then I noticed two gray-haired ladies sitting on a stone bench gazing at the Romanesque Chiesa Santa Maria de Leboreiro. I continued past some stone walls covered with flowers before reaching the medieval Magdalena Bridge over the Rio Seco on the way to Desicabo. I noticed the two women from the bench trying to take each other's pictures by the bridge, so I stopped and offered to take their picture together. They gladly obliged and then took my picture. I stood in front of the arched stone bridge with the purple straps of my backpack pulled tightly around my waist and chest and my fanny pack strapped in front. I smiled, trying to look relaxed.

Horreos outside of Palas de Rei

My next stop, Café Ribeira Sacra, was charming, with an area to order food and drinks and another open area with tables that looked out onto the trail. It felt very welcoming, and wasn't crowded, so I walked inside to order some food and a drink at a counter. But I struggled to communicate that I wanted a sandwich (called a *bocadillo* in Spanish, I discovered). I turned around to see one of the women I'd just taken a picture of standing right next to me. I could tell by her accent that she was British, and I mentioned that I'd hoped to order a sandwich but couldn't explain it to the lady behind the counter. She spoke up immediately and explained in Spanish to the woman what I wanted, and I was handed a menu. I saw a picture of a cheese sandwich on the plastic-covered page, pointed to this, and said, "Cappuccino too." Out of habit, I still reverted to the Italian name for café con leche. The lady seemed to understand now, and I waited there for my order. When it was handed to me, I was amazed by the size of the very long sandwich on crusty French bread. I carried it and my coffee out to the open area and was immediately greeted by the two women.

"Come and sit with us!" they exclaimed.

Happy to oblige them, I did.

One was the retired vicar of a local parish in Bath, England. The other, also retired, was from Shropshire and had worked as a social worker. I asked if they liked the series on BBC called *The Vicar of Dibley,* and they nodded. It was one of their favorites. We shared about our Camino adventures, and they told me how they'd walked it with friends several times. I appreciated their insight, and I enjoyed having someone to sit with over lunch. I took their picture again, this time for me.

My English friends

On the way to Melide, I encountered a gypsy sitting on some steps playing the guitar. Nothing on the trail surprised me anymore. His appearance made my day.

"What else will I see today?" I wondered, loving the serendipity of it all. Melide is a large community of about 9,000 and an important hub on the pilgrimage, according to Brierley. I thought I might find a pharmacy there and spotted one on the busy main street. It turned out to be a parapharmacy, with limited items for sale. I was looking for new toe covers for my blistered big toes and some cortisone cream for my arms that had broken out in a rash after too much sun exposure on the deck of the hotel in Portomarin. I found the toe covers at the parapharmacy, and, a few doors down, a pharmacist at a full pharmacy recommended a special spray for my arms.

On this main street, Rua Progreso, I passed a shoe store and decided to go inside and buy more padded socks. After the three stops, I went to back to an intersection to find where to hook up with the trail. The signage was very confusing. I saw a Camino arrow across the street but could not tell where to join the path. Standing on an island in the middle of the busy street, I turned to see a couple carrying backpacks and obviously walking the Camino.

I yelled to them, "Which way?" and could tell English wasn't their first language, but they pointed me in the right direction. I saw an almost hidden road that led from this main street off between some buildings. The three of us made our way there, and I soon saw others going this way. I was very thankful for their help at that moment.

Ricardo and Christiane were from a small town in southern Brazil. "Rick" was retired and, I guessed, in his 60s, while "Chris" was in her 50s and managed a restaurant. They were walking the entire Camino and then going on to Palma de Mallorca, Spain, and other European destinations. They both wore "Panama Joe" hats, but Chris's rim was pulled up on one side, making her look like an Australian cowboy. Blue-jacketed Rick had a beard, and Chris wore a gray turtleneck and black quilted vest. They both carried aqua-colored backpacks and were very hip-looking and attractive.

They held hands as I took their picture on the rocks that crossed a stone causeway over Rio San Lazaro before we entered a wooded area.

Chris and Rick from Brazil

We passed expansive groves of oak, chestnut, eucalyptus, and pine trees. I never imagined so much natural beauty when I decided to walk the Camino. We spotted a brown cow with her calf, and Chris oohed and aahed over the sight. We both took pictures. A white plaster house with brown trim around the windows and red tiles had a porch in front with pillars decorated with red planters filled with flowering plants. It was an example of the kind of quaint, rural, Spanish houses I encountered and loved. I walked past Igrexa de Santiago de Boente, a white-plaster church with a clock over the door and the usual espadaña—two bells under arches on the roof. The particular beauty of this church was its stone fence topped with lush red flowers and the front gate garnished with many potted pink and red flowers.

We mulled our way through a pretty, wooded, stream-laced area and passed an albergue decorated with red roses. Then we passed a young man sitting by the trail playing an accordion. Again, what would we discover next? He was dressed in shorts and a brown pullover, had long hair and a beard, and wore a pointed hat that made him look like a leprechaun. He reminded me of Phil in the last few years of his life, after the second surgery to remove another tumor-filled lung lobe. He was so full of hope, even after enduring six years of recurring reminders of the lung cancer. Somehow, he was even more magnificent on the guitar. And his voice was so good that John Mayer would have been jealous.

A young man along the trail

After the surgeries, Phil's voice actually improved. While he was in urgent care, after the second surgery, he handed out CDs of his songs, and the nurses praised his music. As soon as he could sing again, he and a younger friend, who beat out a rhythm on a washtub, would perform at local venues in Denver and on Pearl Street in Boulder, Colorado. Theirs was a sort of "roots rock" style that they were proud of. It was unique and very entertaining, and they attracted audiences wherever they went, because they were so good at what they did. I've never heard anything like it before or since. They'd travel to cities where they'd perform outdoors as buskers and drew quite a gathering. Their collections paid the bills.

After he died, I always threw a coin into the hat of any performer or busker I came across...in honor of Phil.

Chris and Rick said goodbye when they decided to stop at an albergue in Castaneda. I wished I could stop there too since my toes were throbbing and my feet ached, but I needed to meet Rachel in Arzua. When I reached the next town, Ribadiso, I stepped into a café on the trail to get a lemon drink and rest my feet for a few minutes. Then I realized how much farther I still needed to go—at least two more miles just to reach the outskirts of Arzua. Argh!

With a population of 6,300, Arzua's modern buildings overshadow its medieval core, according to Brierley. "[It] grew as a town in the 11th century, under the protection of the pilgrimage route, but various archaeological remains and documents show that its birth as a population centre and its importance date from well before the Middle Ages," says *Tourismoarzua .gal*.

Brierley explains that "the noisy central square has a variety of bars, cafés and restaurants and the modern parish church dedicated to St. James with image of Santiago as both Moorslayer and pilgrim. Arzua is known for its local cheese and the cheese fair *festa do queixo* held in March."

I had to find my way around an overpass to a road that went steeply uphill. It was a very tough climb after having walked so many miles already. After reaching the top of the hill, and looking down at a valley, I walked gingerly for what felt like mile after mile and watched for signs of the hotel. I finally saw several albergues popping up along the street and more buildings. I passed by bars where groups of people mingled and realized how late it was—almost 5 pm. I kept walking and looking for Rua de Lugo and almost went down the wrong street when I saw a sign for the hotel. I went straight until I stood right in front of Hostal Restaurante Teodora. I was exhausted. I pushed a door open and went inside.

I found the reception area, where a young man sat behind a counter and talked for what seemed like forever to a Spanish couple who were checking in. I waited patiently to one side, almost hidden from his view, hoping he would see me. He seemed oblivious to my presence and kept talking. On and on. The throbbing in my feet grew so pronounced that I wondered how much longer I could stand there before keeling over. Finally, I stepped around the couple to make sure he could see me.

"Can I help you?" he asked, obviously annoyed that I'd moved to the other side of the couple.

"Oh, yes. I just need to check in," I said.

"Well, you will just have to wait your turn!" he said sharply. "I am helping these people."

"Of course," I responded, taken aback.

I waited patiently. Finally, the couple took their keys and moved toward the elevator to go upstairs.

"Yes?" the young man turned to me curtly.

I gave him my information, trying to be pleasant, as he retrieved my key.

"Thank you," I said, ignoring his discourteous attitude.

I found my bag by the elevator and got in to ride up to my floor. My room was nice with a window that overlooked the street. I was just relieved to be here. I texted Rachel. It was 5:20. She texted back that she had been worried about my whereabouts. When I looked at how many miles I'd walked, it was a total of 18.8 miles. It was the longest day so far.

We went to dinner at a restaurant she'd found across the street, Churreria O Furancho d'Santiso Taperia. I wore my thong sandals to give my feet a break and limped toward our destination. We ordered ribs with a Russian salad, fries, and a bottle of wine that came with the meal. The ribs were super greasy, the salad and fries were ok, but the wine was wonderful!

I was in bed by 8 pm, and I hoped the next two days would not involve quite so much walking. We didn't have much farther to go. Could I do it? What would it be like to arrive in Santiago after coming this far? Would I shout for joy? Would I fall down in front of the cathedral among others and thank God for a safe arrival?

My mind was full, but my body succumbed suddenly to physical fatigue.

"Sweet sleep," I said to myself, and I congratulated myself for making it this far and for covering so many miles in the last three days!

STEP FIFTEEN

RURAL DELIGHTS IN A RUA

*"I am learning another curious lesson: the process of coming to
know people on the camino begins as a matter of chance but
always ends feeling much more like a matter of design."*

—Kevin A. Codd in **To the Field of Stars**

May 20th. Saturday. 11.3 miles to A Rua. At breakfast, I was distracted by a couple at a table near us in the large, crowded hotel dining room. They'd caught my attention at our hotel in Portomarin, when I saw the prominent stickers on their luggage that read "Taiwan." I wanted to hear their story. Why had they come all this way? I assumed they were walking on the Camino. What had attracted them to the pilgrimage?

When I started walking at 8:17, I found the trail down a hill behind the hotel and found myself walking along a wide dirt path through what appeared to be a primeval oak forest. I was especially enchanted as I meandered along several delightful streams. Then I looked ahead and was surprised to see two men dressed in medieval clothing. They were replicating St. James' traditional attire as depicted in the stories and statues of him, with broad-brimmed brown hats donning Camino shells in the front, brown vestments with gourds and leather bags tied around their waists, and brown wool cloaks with red crosses on the lapels over their hearts. Grinning through their thick gray beards and mustaches, they held primitive carved walking sticks in each hand. I picked up my pace to catch up with them and asked if I could take their picture. They nodded. They spoke no English, so I didn't query them with any more questions. Other pilgrims passed by, gawking and pointing. I wondered if the two men represented some organization or endeavor. I later read about others who dress in medieval attire to make the trek in honor of St. James.

Two pilgrims donning medieval attire

"How wonderful and fun," I thought, especially appreciating the up-to-date hiking shoes they wore under the outfits.

I was also pleasantly surprised to find myself walking next to the couple I'd seen that morning at breakfast. I turned and wished them "Buen Camino."

"Are you from Taiwan?" I ventured.

"Yes," the husband acknowledged. "My name is Wu." Then he introduced his wife, whose name I couldn't pronounce or remember, and explained that she spoke no English. She nodded toward me with a bright smile.

"What do you do?" I asked the husband.

"I am a retired orthopedic surgeon," he explained. "I just turned 70 in November."

"That's funny," I said. "I turned 70 in October."

And so, we had an immediate connection.

His wife was 10 years younger than him, just as I am 10 years younger than my husband. It didn't sound like his wife worked, and they had grown children who also lived in Taiwan and had solid professions. I could tell he was very proud of them.

My new friend from Taiwan

"Tell me about Taiwan," I said, and he proceeded to describe the island, once known as Formosa.

"It's about 13,000 square miles and has many beautiful mountain ranges." He explained that they lived near Taipei. I asked if they felt threatened by China, because of recent news I'd heard. His answer stunned me.

"No!" he said adamantly. "China is paper dragon. They roar but we are strong and have plenty of weapons to defend ourselves. We don't fear them."

"That," I thought, "was a different point of view and one I hadn't heard." I wondered then how much of our news is hyped. I was glad to hear this from him. I took their picture, and he insisted on taking one of me with his wife, and I felt her sweetness, even though we didn't understand each other's words. They were both gracious and kind. I felt this very clearly from them.

They moved ahead, and I trekked alone over more medieval pathways with moss-covered stones and cairns, where pilgrims piled mounds of shells, stones, and notes. A yellow and black striped barrel in front of one home displayed walking shoes full of plants. A rack of worn shoes filled with plants and flowers decorated one whole wall. Shelves loaded with "planter shoes" adorned another stone wall along the trail. And the displays made me feel honored to be part of this "gang" of pilgrims who were walking along this common path.

Another shoe planter

At another café, I stopped to rest my feet and eat the remainder of the cheese sandwich I'd saved from the day before. I sat at a table outside in a corner. As I pulled the wrapped sandwich from my backpack, two American couples pulled chairs up to a table next to me. One of the wives complained about her aching, blistered feet, and I detected a Texas accent. I tried to be discreet as I sat behind my small table and propped up my own aching, blistered foot onto my knee and pulled off a shoe. My big toes on both feet were throbbing, and as I pulled off the rubber toe-covers I'd bought, I realized they were causing my toes to hurt even more by constricting the circulation around the large blisters on the outer edges. I pulled the covers off and rebandaged both toes by winding hiking wool around them and securing it with adhesive tape. My toes felt much better!

As I ministered to my feet, I saw that only one man now sat at the table in front of me. The others had gone inside to order lunch. He spoke up and asked where I was from.

"Near Kansas City, Missouri," I answered. "What about you?"

He and his wife were from Iowa, but the other couple were from Texas. They were related. The wives were sisters. I guessed they were in their 60s. When the others returned from ordering, I continued the conversation.

"What do you do?"

The friendly man from Iowa had a dairy farm. The couple from Texas had a ranch, and they'd all decided to walk on the Camino together. I could tell some were enjoying it more than others. We talked about our blisters and shared some stories, but I was anxious to keep walking and could tell they (especially the Texas couple) didn't want to talk. So I wished them well and moved on.

As I emerged from the oak forest and walked uphill toward an open space, I heard someone yelling behind me. I ignored it, thinking the person was calling someone else. But soon I felt a tap on my shoulder. I turned to see the husband of the Spanish couple I'd seen at Casa Benilde the day before. He was very excited and pointed back to his wife and a man walking with her. They caught up to us and I realized this man, Lars from Sweden, who stood at least a head taller than the couple, spoke English and Spanish. And they wanted him to translate for us. Through Lars, I found out that the couple from Barcelona were named Joachin and Pili. They were in their 50s and had one grown son who was in his 20s. When they spoke of him, I couldn't understand their words, but I could tell they had a burden for him. I wasn't sure why or what was going on, but my heart went out to them because I understood how one's love for a son can be weighed down by concerns.

I told them I'd been to Barcelona once. Joachin asked if I'd been to the Sagrada Familia church.

"No," I said. "I wish I had. Maybe one day."

Joachin, me, Pili, and Lars

Lars was very helpful in translating our conversation but seemed anxious to move on. He went ahead, and Joachin pulled up an app to translate between English and Spanish. It was hard to navigate, and we finally gave up. I asked if they were on Facebook. Pili was, so I got her information. As we attempted to converse, I asked why they were walking on the Camino. Pili showed me her hands. I could tell that she had terrible arthritis in her fingers and wanted to be healed. I told her I would pray and placed my hands together to show her. Then I silently prayed. And I thought about all the many reasons for walking this trail you could discover if you just asked each person why they'd come here. Joachin and Pili were such a wonderful couple, and I appreciated all their efforts to communicate with me and how excited they got whenever they saw me on the trail. Their eagerness to see me reminded me of my dogs, who jump up and lick me every time I come in the door. They made me feel altogether appreciated and valued. After this day, I never saw them again. But I hope that someday I will be able to reconnect with them.

Joachin and Pili turned off to go to another town and hotel, and I walked past the Chiesa di Sant'Irene, Irene being an early Christian martyr. I took a picture of the green-doored, rugged-stone chapel topped with an espadaña. It sat alone in a meadow.

Chiesa di Sant'Irene

Farther down the path, I was surprised to see a tiny table beside the trail where a four or five-year-old boy and girl sold painted rocks with messages for the pilgrims. I didn't stop to buy one but wish now I had.

Children selling painted rocks along the trail

Past them, a table was set up along the trail with sheets and a pillow and a sign for "Massages."

"I'd love a good massage," I thought, but felt it would be awkward to lay there beside the path as other pilgrims walked by. A little farther down, I saw the woman masseuse sitting on the ground, ready to offer her services.

"Very resourceful way to help passers-by and make some money," I said to myself.

Phil was always creative in figuring out ways to earn a living. When he moved to Denver after high school to be closer to his dad, he befriended a minister who was referred to him by friends. For years, this kind man acted as Phil's mentor. Richard took Phil under his wing and taught him many skills, including how to work hard and be productive. He showed him how to start his own window-washing business, which ended up being very successful in the years before his death. Before Phil began his business venture, he did odd jobs for Richard. One day, he asked Phil to chop down a dead tree on the side of his house. When Phil completed the task, he told Richard to come and look. When he turned the corner of his house, he gasped. Phil had chopped down the wrong tree! He'd destroyed a live tree.

After Phil's memorial service, Richard invited me to his home and asked me to come around the side of the house to see something. When I came to stand beside him, he pointed at a tall, flourishing tree.

"See this tree?" he said. "It's the one Phil accidentally chopped down!"

From a stump, it had sprung up and grown twice the size it was before. It was beautiful. I thought of how a seed must die before a plant can spring up from it. Life out of death.

A few years ago, I came across something Phil had written about this: "The trees I look at out my window took 30, 40 years to grow mighty and strong. Yet with the simple swing of an axe, their long, tall trunks and branches with leaves flourished by years of rainfall and nourishing minerals, are toppled, slain, and cut to the ground with but a foot-high stump left behind to die in the heat of the noon-day sun. And yet, in spite of the sweltering heat and the dryness, and against all other odds, there are some trees that I have known who fail to die, and begin anew. Yes, there are those trees that live again, and from the center of a corrupted stump begin to reach again toward the heavens, undaunted by obstacles with which they are faced. Unbroken by those who would cut them down. Though pressed with the task of day-by-day growth, these trees shall reach a height greater than previously known."

He wrote this 12 years before he died. It was a prophetic statement about his own life and how, though it might be cut short, he would live on and assume a more spectacular and flourishing life later.

My directions to the hotel in A Rua were a bit obscure. After emerging from a wooded area and finding a small fountain and a sign on a post that read: *Hotel O Pino,* I decided to follow the arrow that pointed toward the road on my right.

"Pretty clear," I thought as I headed up the street. But, as I walked past building after building, I wondered if I was on the right track. As the road dead-ended, I spotted a sign across the street that said, *O Pino Hotel and*

Restaurante. So I made my way up a steep driveway and approached what looked like the entrance.

A Rua is a small, rural village of about 4,359 residents. Before it was taken over by the Romans, who dominated the area between 72 and 195 BCE, it was inhabited by Celtiberians, a group of Celtic people who lived in the central-northeastern Iberian Peninsula. After the Romans, it was under Germanic and Muslim rule, and then the successive rules of Asturias, Galicia, Leon, and Castile. Now, it just seems like a dreamy, quiet hamlet. During my stay at O Pino, I could tell that the hotel's restaurant was an oasis for many locals.

I found the front desk covered with keys waiting to be claimed, and I patiently waited for someone to come and check me in. After I stamped my passport with the hotel's insignia, I noticed an older woman furiously filling orders behind a bar next to the front desk. She yelled something to me in Spanish, and I understood the gist of what she was saying: they were busy and would help me when they could. Finally, a man came over, checked me in, pointed to my suitcase, and gave me my key. There was no elevator, so I lugged my suitcase one step at a time, clambering and banging up three flights.

The hotel was old, but well-kept and clean with a lot of character. White-washed walls were decorated with pictures taken over the years. The description in Mac's app said it was "a small and charming rural hotel that offers 15 comfortable rooms all with heating. The restaurant offers traditional Galician cuisine using the best produce from the land and sea." I found my room at the end of a hallway, after passing a self-service laundry room on the second floor. I opened the door to find two twin beds and a nice large wardrobe inside, and the first thing I did, after throwing my bags down on a bed, was to open my window and gaze down the ancient red tiles to a pretty, shaded lawn surrounded by hedges and trees. A few tables set out with chairs beckoned visitors to come outside and enjoy this exquisite day.

The view from my room at O Pino

I breathed in the view along with some fresh air then turned to pull all my dirty clothes out onto one bed. I looked at my watch to see that I had logged in 12.2 miles. I texted Rachel to let her know I'd arrived and decided that now was the best time to wash as much as I could. My bag full of laundry was bursting! But I had to get some change to operate the washing machine first, so I bounded downstairs to get what I needed and touch base with Rachel, who texted that she was sitting in the restaurant. I found her at a table and sat down across from her. The owner waved his hands and yelled at me, thinking I had cut ahead of a line of people in the bar waiting to be seated. I explained that I just needed to talk to her for a few minutes.

When I looked at her face, I could tell that she was upset. I asked how her day had gone, hoping she'd let me know if something bad had happened. She sighed audibly and told me how, after she'd taken a taxi partway to A Rua and was walking along the trail, she realized that she'd left her phone in the cab. She found someone walking ahead of her who spoke English and asked if they could call the hotel in Arzua so they could contact the taxi driver. The person on the trail was very helpful and was able to reach the hotel and explain the situation. The contact at the hotel said they'd get a hold of the driver, give him her location information, and make arrangements for him to drive out and give her the phone. She waited, the driver showed up with the phone, and she was very thankful for it all ending well. So was I.

"But, how stressful!" I thought. I prayed then for things to go more smoothly. Later, I remembered the dream I'd had the night before we left for France of losing my phone, with my credit cards in it, and how I'd prayed then that God would protect us in every eventuality.

"Thanks, God, for answering that prayer!" I breathed, amazed at His forethought.

After she told me what had happened, and I was assured that she was doing ok, I left to get some change at the bar and start a load of laundry. Next to the laundry room, I found a lovely sitting area with a rocking chair and a couch. I went back to my room and retrieved my Kindle and phone to check messages and read. After a while, Rachel popped her head in and joined me. I went down to the bar and got two glasses of Rioja and some chips and returned to the room. We talked for a while and shared some of our other, better experiences and who we'd met along the way. I finished my laundry and went back to my room to fold clothes and repack my suitcase. I looked at my completely worn out "waterproof" Hokas and decided to leave them here. I had another pair that weren't in such bad shape, and this would give me more space in my suitcase.

I laid down after soaking in the sunshine from my window and taking a shower to freshen up. We met for dinner downstairs around 7 pm and enjoyed the salads, bread, and "Galician fare." I took a picture of a statue of St. James that stood behind the liquor bottles on a shelf behind the bar. It was one of my favorite depictions of the saint. I talked to the owner and found him friendlier and less stressed than when I arrived. And I realized he had little help around the restaurant and relied heavily on the old, cranky woman at the bar.

My favorite St. James statue

That night I asked God if there was anyone He wanted me to talk to the next day.

"Yes," He said. "There will be one."

As I lay in bed, on my side and gazing out the window, I watched as the brightest stars were able to penetrate through the shadowy night sky. And I looked forward to solving this mystery and finding out who it was He wanted me to see.

STEP SIXTEEN

SACRED STEPS TO SANTIAGO

"No matter where you roam on this earth, you will find that the world is smaller than you expected. You will encounter the familiar in the oddest places. You will meet others with whom you somehow already have a connection. It is one of the most wonderful experiences."

—Brian Simmons in **Courage to Conquer**

May 21st. Sunday. Fourteen remaining miles to Santiago de Compostela! It was a pleasant, clear day. Every day this week had started out this way: in the 50s with the temperature climbing up into the 60s, sometimes reaching 70 degrees Fahrenheit. And every day since Alto del Perdon, it had been sunny *and* slightly cool. Perfect weather for walking! And I was very thankful.

I looked one last time at the small fountain on the trail's edge that directed me to A Rua. A ledge built next to it invited pilgrims to sit and rest their weary feet on the flat stones of a small, paved area. It was another reminder of the sacredness of refreshing restfulness and the welcoming hospitality that was enshrined along the pilgrim's way.

Flowered facades along the trail

I passed another stone and plaster-faced home covered with bright red flowers and took a picture to remember all the beautiful flora along the way. I was happy to see that the picture captured two pilgrims walking side by side up the road ahead. Vines grew up so many of the walls and provided leafy shade over the doors and windows of the Spanish homes.

Another small monument stood along the path decorated with the word "Santiago" and a large shell with light radiating from its edges. Pilgrims had carved into areas around the shell with their names. And, at the base, were the usual commemorative stones and shells.

I met a woman as I walked and wondered if she was *the one* God had told me about the night before. She said she was enjoying her life in Naples, Florida, but had spent time in London, where her children were schooled. They had good jobs in Los Angeles now, she said. And she was torn whether to pick up and move closer to them or stay in Naples. She talked about their prestigious lifestyles but never asked about me, my children, or grandchildren.

"Not the one," He said.

Near the town of Amenal, I stopped to use the restroom and get something to drink. As I stood in line, I noticed a carving of St. James near the door. It looked so much like the two men in medieval clothes on the trail. I commented on the resemblance, and other women in line acknowledged they'd seen them too. We all wondered why the men were dressed like St. James. Did they represent a group?

"I thought it was awesome," I said.

After getting a lemon drink, I walked alone up a hill into a forested area. As I entered the ancient hamlet of San Paio, I watched three young women dancing down the road in front of me. They waved their arms and pranced along as if they were celebrating life itself and putting their steps to song. I was fascinated as I watched them, and I wished I had this kind of unsuppressed energy. They continued to go straight as I veered left to follow the Camino signs.

Women dancing down the road

Around a bend I came across a lovely chapel, Igrexa de San Paio de Sabugueira. It stood at the top of a flight of steps, perched as a reminder of the purpose of our pilgrimage, just in case we'd become sidetracked by the people, the views, our excitement to reach Santiago, or our pain.

As I passed by the turquoise church door and looked up at the bell and capella on top, a woman walked past me. We both continued our trek close to each other near a stream and over a bridge. I had a hard time finding the Camino markers when I reached a main road and wandered down the street looking for a sign. Someone in front of a café kindly directed me, and I crossed the street to follow a trail sign on the side of a building. It pointed toward an uphill path that disappeared into a glade of trees. As I passed secluded homes and farms, a small, furry, little black dog captured my imagination. He wandered aimlessly beside me, sniffing as he skirted the dirt path, and I wondered if he was lost. My heart was smitten by him. And I wanted to take him home with me. I thought about how my dogs would love him. He could be part of their "pack." I knew he'd fit in. But I also knew that was a crazy idea. There was no way I could do that. And I felt sad as I moved on.

Farther uphill, I turned to see the woman I'd seen by the chapel. I commented on the dog, and we began to talk. She was from Holland and spoke perfect English. Her name was Yolanda. She was traveling with a group. She said they were "spiritual," but not connected to any church.

"More holistic," she said. "And not very serious about walking."

She smirked as she explained that they were more interested in taking breaks and drinking wine. She was 50 and seriously seeking a way to transition her life to the next stage now that her children were growing up and leaving home. I thought of my daughter, who was the same age and also watching her children prepare to move on with their lives. And I remembered my own feeling of loss when she left home and my son's life ended.

When I asked what she was learning on the journey, she said, "Boundaries."

"How do you mean?" I asked.

She explained how a woman asked to walk with her but then traced her steps so closely that Yolanda thought she'd run into her if she stopped suddenly. Feeling badly, she turned and told the woman that this just wasn't working for her.

"I'm learning how to say no and not feel bad about it," she said.

"So funny! Me too!" I thought about the book I'd just read on the plane. I told her about *Good Boundaries and Goodbyes* and how I was discovering the importance of setting limits and saying no with kindness. She agreed. She'd done this with the group she was traveling with too. And she'd decided that she shouldn't feel bad about walking by herself. She reminded me of my own situation.

I thought about some news I'd seen where a long line of Dutch farmers on tractors were protesting the increased government regulations on agriculture and livestock that were severely impacting their livelihood and their ability to survive.

"What do you think of their protests?" I asked her.

"There are always two sides to every issue," she responded simply. And again, I wondered if we were hearing the whole story on the news.

Then our conversation took a different turn.

"I'm learning more about listening to God," I ventured. "You know, He is light, and is all around us, even in all the things He's made, like the flowers and trees. And He is in us. We can even 'tune into" His voice if we choose to. He wants to speak to us."

She listened and agreed.

"This is the one," God said.

We continued down the trail, and she shared how her husband was struggling with a painful shin. That was why they were walking separately.

"I understand," I said, thinking again about Rachel.

We reached a café near San Marcos and realized how close we were to Santiago. I went to the restroom, and she got in line for a drink. When I came out, I also bought a drink and went to sit at a table outside. I didn't see her at first. So, I ate a tuna sandwich I'd purchased in Amenal and drank my lemon drink alone. Before I left, I saw her at another table and went over to tell her how much I'd enjoyed our conversation.

"I wish you well on the rest of your journey," I smiled.

"You too," she said. And I wonder now if she was able to find the answers she sought.

As I drew closer to Santiago, I said "Buen Camino" to a man as he passed by, and we began a conversation. He was from Austin, Texas, and had walked the entire northern Camino, along Spain's coast, staying in albergues. I asked if he liked to travel this way, and he told me how he'd slept in a bunk bed near a woman who coughed all night. Within three days he started coughing too. He also told me how he'd experienced the hidden blessing of bedbugs. I cringed as he talked, happy we'd decided to stay in hotels.

We passed a small, enclosed area with two tall obelisks, one with the sculpture of a man at the top. Many primitive sculptures surrounded them. At the back stood a deteriorating building with a rusting gate. Propped up on one sculpture, a sign read *En El Camino No hay Carril BiCi.* I had no idea what that meant and kept walking.

I continued down Rua do Peregrino within earshot of Santiago. I grew excited when I passed a huge *Santiago do Compostela* sign. Each letter was colored with messages. Greg offered to take my picture standing next to it. He also used an app to show me how much farther I had to go to get to my hotel. It looked to be right off the trail. I thanked him and he moved on.

In front of a sign close to the destination

I passed by another huge monument with two columns connected at the top by a long metal piece. Bronze 3-D plaques of famous religious figures decorated the sides of one column. I kept going until I saw a sign for my hotel and an arrow that pointed toward some steps on the other side of the street. I crossed over and made my way up the steps to Rua Bonaval. I turned left, quickly found Hotel Alda Bonaval, and was warmly greeted by a young woman behind a counter. She said my luggage was not here yet but gave me a key to number 303. Off by itself, I felt like my room was in the attic. The ceiling slanted down over my bed with an attached skylight that let light in. It was latched shut and the room was stuffy and warm. I figured out how to open it and, when I did, felt a cool breeze rush in. I could hear the loud sounds from the streets below. People talking, cars honking, birds chirping. If I climbed onto a chair, I could gaze out at the slanted, tiled rooftops with chimneys jutting up, and I could see the Old Town with the tall spires of the cathedral in the distance. I sighed. It was spectacular.

Painting of St. James and Santiago de Compostela

I was grateful to lay down my pack and be able to wash my face and hands. After cleaning up, I went back down to the lobby. On the way to the elevator, I a painting by the staircase caught my eye. It depicted St. James standing alone in a meadow, surrounded by plants and trees. Directly behind him, a fog partially eclipsed the Catedral de Santiago. It reminded me so much of our challenging first day on the Camino—the slog and fog we'd endured for so many hours—and all that we'd been through to get here. I almost cried.

The young woman at the front desk showed me a map of how to get to the Pilgrim's Office. I texted Rachel and she messaged back that she'd wait for me at a café near the office. Even with the map, I got terribly lost and went up and down the mostly unmarked alleys, stopping a few kind people who tried to help me, but spoke no English. I found myself growing very frustrated. But what happened next still boggles my mind.

As I stepped around a corner into a colonnade, I was suddenly engulfed by hundreds of people who surrounded me and cheered as a band of young musicians stepped forward to play their instruments loudly and boisterously. To this day, I felt like they were celebrating my arrival and that this was God's way of ceremonially welcoming me to the city. In His own way, He was shouting, "See! You made it! I told you I'd get you through it all and you'd be successful!"

I cried at that moment and realized that, yes, I really was here! And I'd almost made it to my destination. Just a few more steps! I could see the cathedral from a distance...just beyond that building.

I turned another corner and faced a fountain with horses surrounding a pedestal that propped up a woman bearing a star. This was the Plaza de las Platerias, and I was gazing at the Fountain of the Horses, created in 1825 by sculptor J. Pernas. I understand now that the horses represented the strength of life as they spouted water from their mouths, and the woman, holding up the traditional star of Santiago de Compostela, represented the city.

It's customary to throw coins into the fountain, just like the Trevi Fountain in Rome, to show a desire to return here.

Plaza de las Platerias

My son's name, Philip, meant "lover of horses," and I often thought of why we'd branded him with this epithet. Since two of our grandfathers had this name, it seemed appropriate, and we loved the New Testament disciple who followed God's direction and ended up leading an Ethiopian man to the Lord, on a road from Jerusalem to Gaza, and then traveled to many towns sharing the good news. Phil tried to lead a life like this, and I smiled as I thought of the times I'd traveled to visit him in Denver and he'd say, "Let's go!" and we'd drive to a mall and walk around looking for people to talk to so we could share our love for Christ with them. Once we walked up to a young woman at a sales counter. Phil, the outgoing one, began a conversation with her. And he was able to get her phone number since she seemed interested in what he had to share. Then we went to relax and sit across from each other at a brewery and enjoy a beer and talk about life. What a sweet time that was!

I was fascinated by the horse fountain, but still needed to find my way to the Pilgrim's Office. I walked through a tunnel gate that led to Praza do Obradoiro and encountered two buskers playing Celtic music on bagpipes and guitar, and I stopped to listen. It lifted my spirit and reminded me of Phil's busker days.

Greeted by Celtic music

But I was still lost, so I tried to stop a woman who was walking by with hiking poles. Obviously a pilgrim. But she shook her head and waved me away, not wanting to stop and help me. I was saddened and discouraged by this, but I kept going. As I slumped away, I thought "How sad to be so afraid to connect or converse with another person!" Why are some people so paranoid of being approached by someone who is a stranger? This was so unlike the other people I'd met along the Camino, who had, in their own ways, contributed to my healing. A little shook, I turned and took a picture of a statue nearby that depicted Christ on a cross. "Interesting." I thought of the timing of this. Then I ran into a woman coming out of a building.

"Pilgrim's Office?" I asked.

She stopped what she was doing and, not uttering a word, kindly guided me around a corner and pointed down a street. I thanked God for her willingness to help. I nodded and thanked her. And, as I made my way with her directions, I immediately saw where the office was because a long line of people stood outside the door. I walked past it, went further up the street, and looked for a café and Rachel. Then I saw a crowded, umbrella-covered, outdoor eating area attached to a café and spotted the back of her head. I was relieved to see that she had waited. When I went around to face her, I apologized.

"I was so lost!" I sighed. "Sorry it took me so long to get here!"

We tried to order a glass of wine, but the owner gruffly pointed to a sign and told us that we had to order a meal, *then* we could have some wine. We decided instead to go to the Pilgrim's Office so I could get my certificate. A board in front of the office instructed pilgrims to sign in using a QR code. I had no internet service, so Rachel let me use her phone to sign in and fill out what was needed. I showed it to a man at the door, and he pointed for me to get in a line inside. I stood behind many others as we inched along in a row to follow footstep markers on the floor. Rachel stood with me, though she'd already gotten her certificate, and I was happy we could commemorate this moment of achievement together.

Everyone in the room smiled and talked excitedly. All speaking different languages, we cheerfully celebrated this accomplishment together. When I got to the front of the line, I faced a large room with a long counter. People behind the counter politely checked the passport of each pilgrim who came forward. Then I noticed a flashing board on the wall behind them. It announced *Hoy han llegado 1,526 peregrinos,* which meant "Today, 1,526 pilgrims have arrived!" And the number kept going up. I was amazed at the hundreds of people from all over the world who wanted the same experience, each with his or her own reason or desire or hope.

An older man from behind the counter called me up. I was shaking with excitement. He spoke no English, but I was able to make out his words and answer his questions. He used my information on the phone to determine my name then printed my unique Compostela in Latin. After looking at my Camino passport, he decided that I'd at least walked the minimum number of miles from Sarria to Santiago, and I was happy with that. I held up my certificate proudly, thankful to God I'd made it!

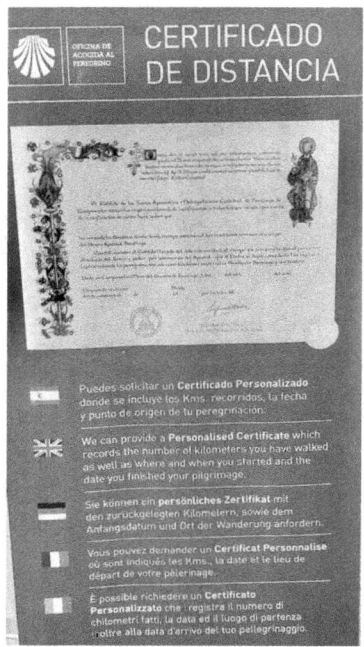

The sign at the entrance of the Pilgrim's Office

On the way back to the hotel, I gazed at a wall sculpture on a building of Mary holding a crowned baby Jesus as she sat on a donkey with Joseph leading them. It depicted their trip into Egypt after the angel warned them to leave Bethlehem. In the background was a palm tree and angels poised above them. I thought about my own journey here and its significance in my life. And I wondered how many angels had hovered over and protected me as I traveled. I was impressed by the volume of artwork throughout the streets and alleys. Another columned building displayed a portico above a beautiful carved door with a sculpture inset of nine people—a mix of women and men being recognized equally. And I thought of how God sees us this way. He doesn't care what sex, nationality, background, or culture we embrace. What matters most to Him is our acknowledgement and trust of Him as we make our way on whatever pilgrimage we've decided to embark on.

As we walked, Rachel shared how, on her way to the Pilgrim's Office, her path crossed that of an older man she recognized. She'd seen him struggling on the trail and had encouraged him by saying he could make it to the cathedral. Now, here he was! He had made it all the way to Santiago! She was elated. She went and congratulated him. And she hoped that her words of support had been the spark he needed to get him here. I thought about her unspoken goal: to help encourage or sustain another's life as her dad had.

"She accomplished what was most important!" I thought to myself.

I was intent on going to the cathedral. But we were both exhausted after all the walking and waiting. Worshipping inside the Catedral de Santiago de Compostela would be a crowning achievement for me. It would offer me a venue to completely lay down the remaining sadness and regret I felt because of my son's death. I desperately wanted to replace these with joy. But now was not the time.

On our walk back through the Old Town

When we got to the hotel, it was 3:15 pm. Our luggage had arrived, and we went to our rooms to shower, rest, and then find a good place to eat dinner. I ministered one last time to my weary feet. Miraculously, the blisters on my big toes were healing nicely and had formed a hard, resilient patch of skin as preparation for future walking pursuits. I still applied salve and moleskin to them and put on my thongs when it was time to go out. We met in the lobby before 5 pm and asked the young woman behind the counter if she could recommend a good place to eat that would be serving this early. She circled a few places on a map that were within walking distance. We set out to find one of the places and walked from Rua Bonaval to Casas Chico. A short way up the alley, we found Pulperia Casas Chico open and stopped for a glass of wine and a bowl of nuts. They were not serving dinner, so we walked outside and saw a man enjoying what looked like a delicious dinner at a table in front of a restaurant. A sign above the door read Bodegon Casas Chico. We were greeted by a friendly man, who was bald with a beard, mustache, glasses, and wearing a bright yellow apron.

"Are you serving food now?" we asked.

"Yes," he responded, and he led us to a table within a little alcove in the restaurant. We were surrounded by shelves full of nicnacs and plaques.

"Very quaint," I thought. "And perfect."

Our waiter at Bodegon Casas Chico

From a menu, I opted for the seafood plate. Of course, with a local red wine. I was surprised when I was presented with a huge bowl filled to the brim with mussels, oysters, scallops, clams, and all manner of shelled seafood. I was in heaven...again! We celebrated by lifting our glasses to toast and felt overjoyed at our arrival. We'd made it!

Not long after being served, a woman in her 60s entered our little enclave. Her name was Carrie, and she lived in Porto, Portugal. She'd moved there from California, joining a group of other expats. She sat at a table next to us, and we relished getting to know her. We asked her many questions, like why she'd come to live in Portugal. Her response was that she wanted to get away from the political upheaval in America. We wondered if she liked living in the area. She nodded and said she made frequent trips to Santiago to shop and eat at restaurants here. This was one of her favorites. We could understand why. We all decided we loved this place.

After becoming satiated with seafood and Rioja, we made our way back up the hill to our hotel and our comfortable rooms. I lay in bed with my skylight open. As I gazed up toward the twinkling, dancing stars above me, I thought about Santiago's *field of stars* and what it really meant. Was it just a symbol of St. James' bones in a field where stars danced above them for a monk? Or was it something deeper? I believed it must mean a lot more than what history revealed.

Bishop Eusebio Elizondo *(nwcatholic.org)* explains it in a beautiful and touching way in *Field of stars:* "[W]hile walking along those large and winding paths [on the Camino], it occurred to me that the "Field of Stars" is the pilgrim Church on earth.... Millions of holy women and men are like those brilliant stars which have established a clear path that guides us along the coasts of heaven to the safe harbor where salvation [wholeness, completion] can be found. Throughout the centuries this constellation of pilgrims has created a milky way by their lives which transmits divine life to us. Some are like distant or small stars whose brilliance can hardly be seen. Others appear briefly in our ecclesial sky, giving us the smallest opportunity to delight in their splendor before they extinguish themselves forever [I thought of my son].... During the long walks I had plenty of time to think and imagine God contemplating from heaven his Church as his "Field of Stars," his "earthly Compostela." Each year, thousands of pilgrims arrive to the tomb of the apostle... before the great heavenly King Jesus, so that his fire may not be extinguished in their lives. Surely the fire of Jesus revives the flame of millions of those stars in his constellation when they draw near to him in order to continue illuminating the dark ravines of this earth where hatred and violence still abound. May your fire, O Lord, burn in our hearts so that your Church may always be your Compostela, your radiant field of stars."

That was it! The field of stars were really the pilgrims who brought His light to the earth, dancing as I once did in a heavenly dream, and raising their hands up to Him in praise.

I listened to the night sounds through my skylight, made up of the traffic and the people below, and I felt like they were all celebrating my arrival and dancing along with me. And I was very thankful to have come this far. But I still hadn't achieved my real purpose—to lay my burden down. And I gave my desire again to God.

"Show me the right time and place," I prayed, wondering what He would come up with this time, since He was always so full of surprises. Would it be at the magnificent cathedral? Or would it happen at a place I never dreamed of?

STEP SEVENTEEN

FINALLY FINISTERE

"It is how we live, how we respond to what life brings us, that creates the difference in our spiritual journey."

—*Joyce Rupp in **Walk in a Relaxed Manner***

May 22nd. Monday. Rachel had signed us up for a bus tour to Finistere (also called Fisterra) and Muxia, where Tom, in *The Way*, went with his friends after completing the Camino de Santiago. Behind the church in Muxia, Tom parted with the remainder of his son's ashes by tossing them into the sea. I remembered this scene and wanted to go there.

The 10-hour bus tour took us first to Ponte Maceira. *Tripadvisor* describes it as a "small, picturesque town on the banks of the Tambre River" and "part of a network of villages known as the most beautiful in Spain.... A 12th century bridge, built on the pillars of a previous Roman bridge, is well-traveled by pilgrims walking the Camino Maritimo to Finistere. A beautiful legend says that disciples of Saint James escaped across the bridge just before it collapsed on their Roman pursuers."

The town was worth the visit, though we only had about 45 minutes to see everything. The bridge offered us stunning views of ancient buildings perched above a waterfall that rippled and burbled down into the river that separated the two sides of the town. A red-tiled stone building, once a mill, sat as a remnant of the past and jutted out over the river, connected to the bridge by a cobbled road.

Muxia is a small fishing village along the Costa da Morte, or "Coast of Death," because so many ships have met their demise here over the years. It was founded on land that belonged to the monks of Moraime, who gave the town its name, *munxia-monxes*. Occupied by Normans in 1105, then Muslims, it was repopulated by King Alfonso VII in 1119. Seeing it as a convenient port, King Carlos of Castile, the Holy Roman Emperor Charles V, purchased it in the 16th century. But it faced destruction by Napoleon's forces in the 19th century. During the 20th century, it survived as a seafaring town with only about 1,000 inhabitants. A tall, white lighthouse watches from its shore, and tourists wander to its seaward side to experience the views. The surrounding rocks are considered magical with curative and prophetic properties.

The lighthouse in Muxia

The Sanctuario da Virxe da Barca, or "Sanctuary of the Virgin of the Boat," also along the shore, is dedicated to the thousands of pilgrims who travel from Santiago to Muxia. Legend says it sits at the place where the Virgin Mary arrived in a stone boat to encourage St. James to preach throughout Galicia. Rebuilt several times, lastly in 2015, it's decorated in a nautical theme. I peeked inside then wandered down below the church to see the large boulders where Tom stood to toss his son's ashes into the sea.

A surprising, shockingly out of place, sculpture caught my eye as I emerged from the shore. Called *A Ferida*, or "The Wound," and created by sculptor Alberto Bañuelos Fournier, the 36-foot-tall granite statue looks like lightning or something being ripped apart. It was donated to the Muxians as a memorial to the volunteers who came to help the Galicians when the Prestige oil spill occurred on November 13, 2002. I stopped and gazed at it, reminded of my own wound, still lingering, and how much I needed to be free of it.

A Ferida, "The Wound"

A tall pedestal with a crucifix drew my attention so I walked across the road to take a look. But my eyes were pulled in another direction as I noticed people walking toward a towering hill. The narrow trail they ascended beckoned to me. So I fell in line behind them to climb to the top of Mount Corpino. As I came over the summit, I discovered a breathtaking view of an estuary. Cape Vilan sat on the opposite shore, along with the beautiful beaches of Leis and O Lago.

But then my eyes landed like a dove on something even more intriguing. A lone cross sat solidly perched on top of a large rock just below me. Shells and stones covered its base and sparkled in the sun like tearful winks. Not hesitating, I reached deep inside my backpack and retrieved the scallop shell I'd saved. Holding it for the last time, I turned it over and read the inscription on the inside: "James 1:12."

"So perfect for St. James and for my son!" My eyes watered as I thought about the meaning: *"God will bless you, if you don't give up when your faith is being tested. He will reward you with a glorious life, just as he rewards everyone who loves him" (Contemporary English Version)*. It reminded me of how Phil never forsook his belief and trusted God to the very end, even as his body melted away like butter on a hot stove. And I smiled when I thought about how, one day, I'd see him living this glorious life God had promised him. And we'd both fly away from hills like this one to search out new and more beautiful mountain views.

I shimmied down the steep hill to stand next to the cross. I brushed away sand on the base to create a special spot among the other memories. I whispered a thank-you to God for my son's life and what it meant to me and how he'd touched so many people. Then I remembered Phil's words before he died: *"It's not the body [the outer shell] that's most important. It's the spirit inside you that will live on."*

"This is for you, Phil." I carefully placed my shell in the empty spot at the base of the cross. And, at that moment, I realized that he was in a much better place than I was and that, though he'd never journeyed to places like

I had and seen scenes like this one, what he was viewing was far superior to anything I could ever envision in this life. And he was at peace. And experiencing a heaven I would one day see but could not even imagine now.

At that moment, I felt like I was grasping the fringe of my journey's quest. I gazed out at the blue mountains on the other shore. The clouds that had hovered above them now dissipated so I could see more of the sun and the sky. And I looked down at the shell laying there on the rock, holding the regrets for me, like water once scooped up by pilgrim scallops.

The cross in Muxia

After visiting Finisterre, once considered the end of the known world, we bussed our way to the Fervenza do Ezaro waterfall, the world's largest horreo in Carnota, and Santa Maria do Campo church in A Coruña. As I gazed at the spectacular waterfall, I remembered a dream I'd had shortly before Phil died. It was so vivid and real that it left an unforgettable impression on me. In the dream, Phil motioned to me to leave a family gathering and go with him over a waterfall and down a fast-moving river. Together, we dove over the fall, without a raft or a boat, down the rushing rapids. We zoomed past people and laughed as we waved to them. Then we stood on a cliff overlooking a magnificent, lush valley filled with beautiful trees and a stream running through it.

"Let's go!" he shouted. And we took off, soaring through the air like giant birds over the trees.

"Let's stop there!" he pointed toward a large log building on top of a forested mountain. We flew toward it and walked inside to be greeted by a group of people in the entryway. They were dancing enthusiastically and singing with waving hands raised. We joined in, and I whirled around them, swinging a long, multi-colored skirt that captured all the colors of the rainbow. I remembered how God had once shown me that my life was multi-faceted like a diamond and multi-colored like a rainbow.

We walked into another room, where a man behind a bar pulled a tap to fill pilsner-style glasses with some sort of "brew."

"Do you want some?" he asked smiling.

"Sure," we both responded. And he handed us foamy drinks that tasted like sweet ambrosia or honey. We sat together at a wooden table and enjoyed our beverages as we looked around. It was fabulous. It reminded me of all the times we'd sit together enjoying a beer and talking about life.

Suddenly, Phil said, "Let's go!" and we birled and flew out the door to explore more of this amazing new world. When I woke up, it dawned on me that we were experiencing paradise. This is what our future together would look like! God had given me this scintillating vision to bring me encouragement and hope during the dark days of uncertainty and death.

When we returned to Santiago, we capped the day by returning to Bodegón Casas Chico. We were thrilled to find our friend Carrie, sitting in the same small enclave. This time I ordered a cheese board covered with European taste-samples. Rachel and Carrie savored the shrimp soup. We slept well that night after such a long trip. I decided I much preferred walking versus sitting on a bus all day. And I was relieved that I'd found the right place to lay down what had been on my mind for so long. But I still felt like I had more to unload. The shell held my regrets, but my heart still ached.

On the Camino, I'd seen God work through events and serendipitous interactions to bring me needed healing all along the way—mentally, spiritually, and physically. But what about my greatest challenge—to completely lay down the pain surrounding my son's death? Like a mountain made out of a molehill, it was constructed from layers of hurtful words spoken. I felt like these raw remnants were little bitty crumbs that kept appearing to entice me toward a deadly mouse-trap. And I wondered if a visit to the cathedral would finally rid me of these pests.

Step Eighteen

Adios Amigos

"The Camino de Santiago gives birth to another pilgrim the moment he heads for home. And thus, as the walking's done, the real journey begins."

—*Steve Watkins in* **Pilgrim Strong**

May 23rd. Tuesday. After breakfast, we headed for the Catedral of Santiago. As we approached the huge, multi-faceted church, I realized that my first impression, when I saw the "horse fountain" on Plaza de las Platerias and the steps that led to huge green doors under arches, had been the actual pilgrim entrance.

The main cathedral entrance, on Praza do Obredeiro, has a grand Renaissance-style, diamond-shaped staircase and entryway. But it's been blocked by a metal gate since 2015. Looking at it now, I was overwhelmed by the cathedral's front: two elaborate towers stand on either side of a main central tower that's topped by a statue of St. James wearing pilgrim garb and looking down from an arch.

Back to Plaza de las Platerias, we entered through the green doors and approached the altar from the back of the nave. With a mass in progress, and we tiptoed alongside the main aisle to find seats in a side aisle, or transept. I found the elaborate gold designs that surround the arched high altar jaw-dropping. A gold effigy of St. James stands near the bottom of the altar and, in front of him, the famous, giant incense burner hangs expectantly. The five-foot-tall *botafumeiro* is swung from the center of the church across both transepts that create the shape of a crucifix across the nave. The tradition is only performed on special days, and we knew we would miss this inexplicable experience. But we decided to stay long enough to appreciate the views within the church and listen to the music and chanted words of the priest.

As I sat there, I prayed again for complete release from pain. Then I remembered an odd dream I'd had a few years back. I was on vacation with my family, and, when we got back to our hotel after walking along a beach, I went to retrieve clothes from my suitcase and found it filled with dead leaves! I grew more and more frustrated and upset as I dug my fingers through the gritty pile to get to my clothes. And then I had to pick off the crumbling leaf-bits from every single thing I pulled out. As I dug underneath the debris, I was shocked to find a brand-new bathing suit at the very bottom! I pulled it out, shook off the "dross," and decided to try it on. But I wondered, "How did it get here?"

Baffled, I woke up and asked God what this dream meant. His answer? "The dead leaves are hurtful memories you need to shake off. They're causing you too much pain. I never meant for you to keep experiencing so much sadness. When I made people, I wanted them to live and enjoy the earth's bounty with joy and thankfulness. Sadly, My adversary entered the garden and expropriated My gifts. Now, many lives are cut short, and I mourn to see the devastation that results from the enemy's deception. One day, this will all change when My Son returns to form a new world, where people can live as I intended...forever. Until then, replace the dead leaves, or sad thoughts, with what I've clothed you with, the joy of My Spirit. Like the new bathing suit, this gift can bring you peace and healing if you'll live in it! It can make you into a new person if you'll let it. Through its power, you can remove the dead past and experience newness of life. I love you."

And I thought of a verse I loved in Philippians 3:13 that says, *"forgetting what lies behind and straining forward to what lies ahead"* (*The Amplified Bible*).

"What *does* lie ahead," I wondered. "Well, I guess I can look forward to finding out!"

As I lingered in the cathedral, I visually lifted the painful memories...one at a time all the way up to God. They were His now to do with as He chose. And I knew what He *would* do with them. He'd blow them away like broken leaf bits, as far away as possible, just as I should've done so many years before, but just couldn't.

Being present for a service in the cathedral cemented my reason for coming to Santiago. It created an anchor for my journey here. I felt like I could sigh now, knowing that I'd completely laid it all down. I'd mentally and physically left my regrets in the shell at the foot of the Muxia cross overlooking the sea. But now, my heart and my spirit felt lighter because I'd spiritually raised up the remaining regret-shreds to the One Who stood over this altar, this church, this city, this earth. And I'd left them in His hands. I was now anchored in peace and my sails were lifted with joy because I'd lightened my load. I could now sail through the rest of my life-journey unencumbered. My heart was completely empty of leaf-bits. But full of His Spirit.

We spent the rest of the morning happily investigating many of the Camino-related shops near the cathedral. Then, of course, more coffee and lunch in the cute cafés. One was decorated in a nautical theme, like the church in Muxia. From a corner, we enjoyed watching customers come in and out. Most were familiar to the people who worked there. One older man in a tweed jacket, obviously a frequent visitor, sat alone by a window watching passersby. I wondered what his story was. He seemed so contemplative and reminded me of a famous author. So wistful was his gaze! I was sure he had an interesting history.

Last views toward the cathedral

We made our way back to the hotel for a 2:30 pm pickup and ride to Vigo, where we'd stay the night before leaving on an early morning flight to Madrid. We waited by the front door for at least a half hour. No one came. The young lady at the front desk called and got another driver to come at 3 pm. The first driver had been delayed, she said. We hopped into the taxi for the hour and a half drive. Our hotel, Agua Del Mar, turned out to be quite nice, though the city seemed very industrial. It was a little gem in the middle of a lot of hustle and bustle, contemporary with wonderful rooms and bathrooms.

We checked in, cleaned up, then met back downstairs for a cocktail in the reception area. The young woman who checked us in also acted as a bartender and made a very strong gin and tonic for me. I guessed it was the first one she'd ever made. We sat on a comfortable couch near the front window, eating nuts and sipping our drinks. Then we headed out to a busy, pedestrian-packed street. People bobbed in and out of stores and rushed to the corners to wait for the lights to change. I watched and thought wistfully of our wonderful days walking in the Spanish countryside. How I missed the quiet serenity!

We found an outdoor table with an umbrella and ordered food and wine. Two ladies with a dog next to us made helpful recommendations. Spaghetti and salad sounded good to me. I enjoyed just sitting and eating a savory dish as a cool breeze wafted through and we waited for the sun to set.

A taxi arrived the next morning at 5:30, and we arrived in plenty of time for an 8 am flight. We even had to wait for the ticket counter to open. Traveling through Madrid, we caught our flight to Atlanta, then to Kansas City. We were home by 5:40 pm.

On the first flight, I wrote in my journal one last time. At the top of the page I wrote, *The Camino Connection*, then, "In a world driven to isolation as super-interconnectivity forces many to a lonelier existence, the Camino offers a special place of real connection. As I sit on the plane from Vigo to Madrid, where I can get on another plane bound for home, I am struck by how the young man next to me, unlike so many on the trail, has 'tuned out' and resists any attempt to connect to a fellow passenger by immediately plugging in his ear buds. His music, loud enough for me to hear two seats over, reminds me that he is resistant to me. It drowns out the sounds of people and other things around him. His eyes avert mine, and he is always looking out the window. And I think of how different my experience for the past two weeks walking the Camino de Santiago has been."

It has changed my life.

In a world marked by mental distance, family separations, divisions between communities, states, nations, and individuals, and spiritual severance, even within churches, how relevant is a place where one can go and find a common bond that surpasses nationality, ethnicity, language, background, wealth, and position? I found that place while walking a dirt-covered trail between rows of red poppies and grapevines and cobbled lanes past stone-faced churches with arch-covered bells that rang when the moment was right. I felt rain on my face and wind at my back. I climbed up and down and over rock-covered hills and made my way through eucalyptus forests between moss-covered stony fences. I watched as sheep peacefully chewed in pastures and dogs lay gazing at passing trekkers. I heard horses neighing and roosters crowing early in the morning as the world woke up and went happily on in the Spanish countryside. I engaged with women and men from England, Canada, Taiwan, America, New Zealand, Sweden, Italy, Bulgaria, Spain, Ireland, Germany, Wales, Brazil, Holland, and other countries. I was enthralled by the gilded interiors of large cathedrals and touched by the rusticity of small rural churches that were covered with thick, green vines. I tasted fried squid, fresh-baked bread, local cheeses, seafood-loaded paella, salads with anchovies, sardines, and salmon that were covered with white asparagus, cucumbers, olives, local lettuce, and tomatoes, croquetas full of ham and cheese, a variety of tapas, and many regional red wines. I walked between six and 19 miles a day and survived the toughest treks through painful blisters and aching feet. I gazed down cliffs to see spectacular scenes by the sea and ambled across ancient Roman bridges that crossed over burbling, bubbling brooks. And I often wondered how many pilgrims had passed this way. But, by far, it was the people I met along the way who helped me to heal.

The Camino taught me that life is never what you thought it would be, so you make something special out of what you are given. Today, I look again at the shell I found while walking before I left for Spain, and I am still amazed at how God made it so clear in a most unique way that *"I can do all things through Christ who strengthens me"* (Philippians 4:13). It was that verse that got me through the hardest days and reminded me that He is in it all, even the painful times, and can bring needed healing.

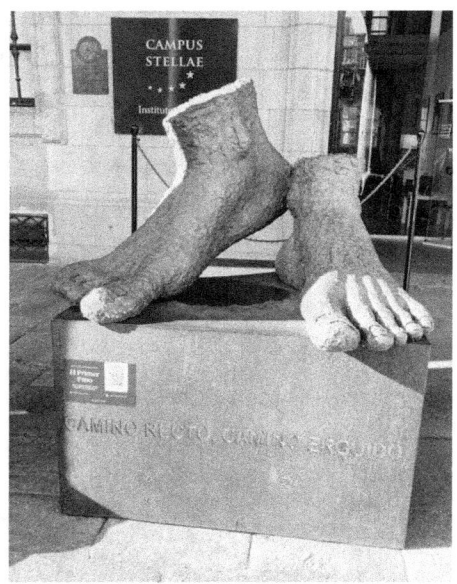

A monument to pilgrims in Santiago

If you enjoyed the book, please leave a review:

linktr.ee/authorlelebeutel

The Beatitudes of the Pilgrim

Blessed are you, pilgrim, if you discover that the Camino opens your eyes to what is not seen.

Blessed are you, pilgrim, if what concerns you most is not to arrive, but to arrive with others.

Blessed are you, pilgrim, when you contemplate the Camino and you discover it is full of names and dawns.

Blessed are you, pilgrim, because you have discovered that the authentic Camino begins when it is completed.

Blessed are you, pilgrim, if you discover that one step back to help another is more valuable than a hundred forward without seeing who or what is by your side. Blessed are you, pilgrim, when you don't have words to give thanks for everything that surprises you at every twist and turn along the way.

Blessed are you, pilgrim, if you search for the truth and make of the Camino a life of your life.

Blessed are you, pilgrim, if on the way you meet yourself and gift yourself with time, without rushing, so as not to disregard the image in your heart.

Blessed are you, pilgrim, if you discover that the Camino holds a lot of silence; and the silence of prayer, and the prayer of meeting God, who is waiting for you.

—from ***Buen Camino, What a Hike through Spain Taught Me about Investing and Life***
by Gordon J. Bernhardt

The Pilgrims' Prayer

Although I may have traveled all the roads, crossed mountains and valleys from East to West, if I have not discovered the freedom to be myself, I have arrived nowhere.

Although I may have shared all of my possessions with people of other languages and cultures; made friends with Pilgrims of a thousand paths, or shared albergues with saints and princes, if I am not capable of forgiving my neighbor tomorrow, I have arrived nowhere.

Although I may have carried my pack from beginning to end and waited for every Pilgrim in need of encouragement, or given my bed to one who arrived later than I, given my bottle of water in exchange for nothing; if upon returning to my home and work, I am not able to create brotherhood or to make happiness, peace and unity, I have arrived nowhere.

Although I may have had food and water each day, and enjoyed a roof and shower every night; or may have had my injuries well attended, if I have not discovered in all that the love of God, I have arrived nowhere.

Although I may have seen all the monuments and contemplated the best sunsets; although I may have learned a greeting in every language, or tasted the clean water from every fountain; if I have not discovered who is the author of so much free beauty and so much peace, I have arrived nowhere.

If from today I do not continue walking on your path searching and living according to what I have learned; if from today I do not see in every person, friend or foe a companion on the Camino; if from today I cannot recognize God, the God of Jesus of Nazareth as the one God of my life, I have arrived nowhere.

— from *Senior Camino* by *Donald Bowes*

AFTERWORD

"Roughly speaking, there are three kinds of people. You have the walkers who look on it as a challenge, a physical challenge. You have those who do it for reasons of faith. And then you have the pilgrims. The pilgrim never knows why he is on the path. And the path doesn't go to Santiago—you always stay on the path. It's people who are always searching for something. Once you are a pilgrim, you stay a pilgrim."

—Jeannick in **Pilgrim Strong** by Steve Watkins

I tried to keep my poise and balance as I stepped precariously up the stairs onto the stage in my new, black, high-heeled shoes. I did *not* want to trip and fall in front of this crowd made up of all my colleagues. I was retiring, and this was my last company banquet and my moment to give any last-minute, inspiring thoughts to sum up my 25 years as a financial advisor. I clomped my way across the platform to the podium and reached up to adjust the microphone.

"I'm short," I quipped.

Then I explained that I'm a better writer than speaker and how I'd written a few words about my recent journey, which some of them had heard about.

"It has to do with you!" I promised. "I call it *The Camino Connection*."

And so I began: "Maybe you're starting to see how this world is really a very small space! Recently I came across a quote in a devotional that read: "You are being led out into a larger place." And I watched to see how this might happen. At last year's summer regional meeting, Rachel expressed a desire to walk the Camino de Santiago. As many of you know, we actually did it! We walked part of the Camino this past May. The traditional Camino is a 500-mile pilgrimage that goes from St. Jean Pied de Port, France, to Santiago de Compostela, Spain. Known as *The Way of St. James,* it's a well-known journey where pilgrims lay down a personal burden at the feet of St. James in a cathedral that honors his own journey there.

"Every Camino trekker has a goal. Some make the journey for physical reasons, maybe to accomplish a walking goal. Others go for mental objectives, like figuring out a life transition or overcoming a life challenge. Many make the trek for spiritual reasons, like healing or getting closer to God. Mine was all three. And all three reasons were answered in ways I could never have imagined.

"But the 'extra' I experienced was through the amazing people I met along the way. You see, besides getting up early each morning to the sounds of roosters crowing, cows lowing, horses neighing, dogs barking, and birds twittering, there was the sight of hundreds of pilgrims walking along a trail, sometimes through the mist, all in a line and on the same journey.

In the mornings, no one uttered a sound. We all walked in silence through fragrant eucalyptus forests, past red-poppy-filled and grape-vined fields, up and down rocky, graveled paths past manured pastures, over brook-traversing bridges, past ancient stone-faced buildings and churches covered with vines, and barns filled with sweet-smelling hay. As the morning progressed, cafés popped up along the trail, and many of us stopped for a fresh-brewed cup of coffee and a crusty croissant. Then the conversations began.

"We first met John from Seattle and Mark from Houston, who walked together. Then David from Wales, who shared stories about his home and how he celebrated retirement by living out his dream of walking the Camino. Seventy-four-year-old Sylvia from Sweden set out on the pilgrimage every year as a gift to herself. Three sisters from Italy, who spoke very little English, shared what they could about their journey together. Two retired women from Britain, one a vicar and one a homemaker, asked me to join them for coffee at one café stop, and they shared about their lives in Shropshire and Bath. Wu and his wife talked as we walked about life in Taiwan. Pili and Joachin from Barcelona showed up at the same stops along the way. They spoke no English but found a translator in Lars from Sweden to tell me that their pilgrimage meant healing for Pili's arthritic hands. Ricardo and Christiane from Brazil helped me find the right path, when the signs were confusing, then walked with me to the next town. Fifty-year-old Yolanda from Holland shared how she was trying to figure out what came next for her as her kids left home one by one. And Greg from Austin told me about his experiences staying at the albergues along the way.

"Every one had a story, every one had a dream, every one had a reason to be there. And the draw for us all was connection—something that could never be made over the internet or through TV or by talking on the phone. It was something that could only be done in person, face to face with life. In a super-connected world, where answers and things can be had at the touch of a button, they saw that true value lies in heart-pounding, body-sweating, cobblestone-jostling, hiking-pole-extending, croissant-savoring, rooster-crowing, poppy-smelling, coffee-cultivating, eye-tearing moments like those on the Camino. No media could ever give them this, and they knew it!

"And that is why you are different. That is why what you offer means so much to the people you serve, who savor real-life, meaningful connections so they can know and feel that they are reaching their life goals. You are truly different. What you do means so much more than you can imagine. Why? Because you can touch and hear and see and discern the hearts and souls of the people who come to you. Never forget this! Remember it today. Remember it tomorrow. Remember it the next day. You are different because you can connect to life face to face. And you must reach out to see how you are being led from a small space into a very large place."

I ended my speech with "Thank you!" and made my way back off the stage, my mind reeling with memories of my years as an advisor, but, even more so, of the more recent life-changing days I'd spent making my way across many miles with people from all over the world. And the eternal impact of each person along the way.

THE CAMINO CONNECTIONS CONTINUE...

"Wherever you are, whatever you're doing, you must pick up the trail and follow the map you have at hand."

—*John Eldredge in* **Restoration Year**

The Camino has not ended for me. I guess I'm still a pilgrim and always will be. I'm still experiencing ongoing connections as a result of my journey! Here are some examples....

Mary....

The other day, while walking Barney around a lake near my house, a woman I'd met months earlier stopped me. She knew that I'd walked on the Camino de Santiago.

"Did you know a lady up the street from me is getting ready to walk on the Camino too?" she asked.

"No," I responded. She didn't give me her neighbor's name, and I wasn't sure if I'd ever meet her.

A week or so later I spotted a woman I'd seen before walking. This time she was wearing a backpack.

"That must be her!" I thought.

The next week, early in the morning, I suddenly faced her coming toward me down the street. I stopped her as she passed by.

"Are you walking on the Camino de Santiago?" I ventured.

"Yes!" Her eyes opened wide with surprise.

"I just walked it last May!" I exclaimed.

"Oh, wow! I'm going with my son in two weeks," she said, excited.

"I have a small book called the Michelin guide that has great maps," I said. "I didn't get it until after I returned, and it would have been so helpful. I'll bring it to you tomorrow." I hoped to see her at the same time and place the next day.

"Great. Thanks. I don't have that."

"I'll also write down my name and phone number. I'd love to hear about your adventure when you get back!"

"That'd be great. By the way, my name is Mary."

"You remind me so much of a Mary I once knew."

"Yes, I know. We used to work together! I remember you!"

Now, my eyes popped open.

"Oh my gosh, I wondered if you were that Mary, but I didn't think you lived in this area."

"Yes, I moved here a few years ago."

"Small world!" I thought, totally amazed.

She was my manager in a former job, 27 years ago, where the work environment was unforgiving, and I often felt overwhelmed. On my long drive to and from the office every day, my stomach churned, and I developed frequent migraines and dizzy spells. After I left for another job, I wondered how she survived in that place. She was a thoughtful person trying to manage a group of young people in a very challenging department. And I realized that God had set up this encounter so I could reconnect with her as a friend who also sought a deeper and more spiritual life experience. She mentioned her son, who was now the age of mine when he died. She didn't know this. Her son had been five years old when I knew her before. I was happy she still had her son and could experience with him what I wanted so much to do with my own son. And, one day, I'd tell her about Phil.

Israel...

Since retirement, My husband and I have started an annual tradition of driving to a place we've never been where we can bring our dogs along for the ride. Last year, we drove to Sister Bay, Wisconsin, stayed in a dog-friendly inn on the water, and enjoyed hiking and sailing with them. We loved it!

This year, we drove to Albuquerque, New Mexico, to watch the annual Balloon Festival in October. While traveling from Missouri to New Mexico, we stopped in Hays, Kansas, at one of our favorite places, Gella's Diner and LB Brewing. It just so happened that when we arrived for a late lunch, I ran into a waiter we'd connected with years before on one of our trips to Denver to visit grandkids. I was so excited to see Israel and brought him over to see my husband. We talked for a while, and I mentioned I'd walked on the Camino in May.

"Do you know about the Camino de Santiago?" I asked.

"Yes!" he responded. "I've walked the Camino two times!"

"Oh my gosh! Really? What inspired you to go?" I asked.

"The last time was over a year ago," he explained. "I wanted to go with my wife. We were having some marital problems and lacked a clear focus of what to do. We had our separate goals and needed to find a way to be unified in what we wanted to see happen in our lives."

"Did you discover what you were looking for while you walked?"

"Yes. We did. We were able to sort out what we wanted to see happen and agree on how we'd achieve it. We decided that I'd keep working here at Gella's while she pursued her master's degree. Then, when she completed her studies and could work in her chosen field, I'd go after my dream of starting my own restaurant. She finished her degree this year and I'm

opening my own Mexican restaurant here in Hays in the next few months."
He smiled.

"What a wonderful story!" I exclaimed. It was another testimony to me
of what this journey can do for those who decide to accept the challenge.
Israel and his wife had gone for the purpose of clarification, and they found
a way to achieve what they needed and wanted.

Mike...

My husband, Mike, did not go with me on the Camino because his
legs bother him if he stands or walks for too long. He worked on his feet
for years and has had many vein surgeries. After walking the Camino, I
explained how different this trip was compared to the bus trips and cruises
we'd always taken.

"You see so much more," I tried to explain. "Instead of riding on a bus
or boat for hours and days, then experiencing a place for 45 minutes or a
few hours, then hopping back on the bus or boat, you're immersed in a
place. You see and breathe and feel the interior of a location. You meet the
people. You experience the culture."

I wanted so much for him to at least partially experience what I had
on the Camino. I looked into walking tours we could do and found
one through Mac's Adventures to the Cotswolds in England, where we
wouldn't need to walk as far and could take breaks when needed. I showed
him the pictures and asked if he'd be interested. The more I talked about
the possibility, the more excited he became. Now, we're planning a trip and
will see how it goes. My hope is that every year we can do a walking trip to
places we've never been...all because of my experience on the Camino.

Almost every week, I run into people who ask about my journey. They
either just want to hear about it, or they aspire to walk it themselves and
wonder if they can. So many are people my age who suffer from hip and
knee and joint pains and think it would be an unlikely attempt. But I think
about Sylvia from Sweden who, at 74, walks it every year. Or the man I

saw on the trail walking with a bandaged knee. Or David from Wales who made this his retirement goal. So many unlikely people have done it! But I do recommend to everyone I talk to that they make sure they prepare for it by walking...a lot! And to do it while they can. If God is putting it on your heart, consider how you *can* do it.

The *The Amplified Bible* version of Philippians 4:13 reads: *"I have strength for all things in Christ Who empowers me [I am ready for anything and equal to anything through Him Who infuses inner strength into me; I am self-sufficient in Christ's sufficiency.]"*

It will be worth it. *I promise.*

ALBERGUES OR HOTELS?

Albergues come in many shapes and sizes. These hostel-like inns can be modern and include clean, private rooms and bathrooms, but most have large rooms filled with bunkbeds or mats on the floor. And everyone usually shares the same bathrooms and showers. You must get used to sleeping next to all manner of pilgrims, and some could be carrying bedbugs or other kinds of bugs. They could cough or snore all night. Costs for public albergues range from 8-10 euros per night; a bed in a private room averages 12-15 euros. Host-owners can be very hospitable and friendly, while others are very business-like and gruff. Pilgrims who travel from albergue to albergue have more flexibility because they can begin looking for a place with available beds when they grow weary and need to rest. They also carry all their belongings in their backpack, with the recommended load being no more than 10 percent of your body weight. This is convenient because they have everything with them and don't need to worry about their luggage getting to the next place. But they must trek with this extra weight every day. And hope they can find an albergue when they need one. I have read that, as you draw closer to Santiago, it's harder to find a place with available beds. Many people swear that this is the true way to journey across the Camino if you want the authentic pilgrim experience. Sometimes I wish I had traveled this way to get an even more life-changing experience overall.

Booking hotels or paradors is another way to travel. The average cost for a budget hotel in Spain is between $30 and $50 per night. Paradors are government-run businesses "that turn historic castles, convents, monasteries, and other buildings into luxury hotels," says Reginald Spittle, in his book *Camino Sunrise*. "The most famous is next to the cathedral in Santiago." We chose to stay in hotels because, after walking many miles each day, we knew we'd want the assurance of a private room with a bathroom where we could rest, relax, and clean up, and have laundry services available. I'm a light sleeper, and I knew I'd get no rest if someone nearby was snoring or coughing. I also did not relish the idea of sharing a bathroom or the bedbugs and germs that come with the albergue experience. I would have liked getting to know more people along the way in the rooms and at meals and having more opportunities to bond with other walkers, like Tom did in *The Way*. But I did appreciate that I always knew I had arranged lodging, and I could go directly to my own room, where I could gaze out a window, breathe in the views, and have some alone time to read and check messages. It was especially nice at the end of a long and grueling day of walking beside many other people.

We used a transportation service to move our luggage from one hotel to the next so that we only needed to carry a light backpack during the day. This was a great relief but necessitated that we arrive at the next planned location by the end of each day. Because of this, we had less flexibility than pilgrims who carry everything with them and have no reservations.

Some people do a combination of staying in albergues and hotels. They might mostly stay in albergues but decide to splurge a night or two in a nice hotel. In *The Way*, Tom and his friends did this. It's really whatever works best for you.

Most people want to walk the entire Camino. If you have the time and can take about 35 days off, this is ideal. I wish we could do this, but neither of us had that much time available. So, we opted to take two weeks and walk the first and last parts of the Camino. This worked for us. We also opted to take taxis some days because of aches and pains or terribly inclement weather. Some consider this anathema and look down on those who would consider traveling as a pilgrim in this way. Remember, it's your Camino, and, if you need extra help along the way, but still want to complete the journey, don't let your own or anyone else's attitude stop you. Just do the best you can. I've done it both ways. I've used a taxi when needed, and I've also walked the whole way between Sarria and Santiago to experience the Camino as much as I could.

Good Camino-related books

Here are a few helpful and inspiring books from authors who walked the Camino de Santiago....

I'll Push You, a Journey of 500 Miles, Two Friends, and One Wheelchair *by Patrick Gray and Justin Skeesuck.* Two childhood friends, now adults, decide to tackle the Camino. The only issue is that one has a neuromuscular disease that robs him of the use of his arms and legs. No problem! His friend commits to pushing him in a wheelchair over the entire 500 miles. With the help of other pilgrims, they complete the journey. A miraculous feat! And an inspiring account.

Walking with Sam, a Father, a Son, and Five Hundred Miles Across Spain *by Andrew McCarthy.* This book is about a father, who remembers his own life-changing teen experience of walking the Camino, and he wants to share the experience with his teenage son. Entertaining and funny, it grows more meaningful as their divergent views end up coming together along the way.

To the Field of Stars *by Kevin A. Codd.* This thoughtful account by a priest walking the Camino Francés to Santiago meaningfully describes his encounters and adventures. It is thought-provoking and insightful and one of my favorites.

Beyond the Field of Stars *by Kevin A. Codd.* Taking the Camino a step further by trekking from Belgium to Santiago, the author, confronted by physical challenges, shares how friends step up to help him overcome each new ordeal. As in his first book, his faith, insight, and luminous way of looking at every encounter make this book as meaningful and enlightening as his first book.

Walk in a Relaxed Manner: Life Lessons from the Camino *by Joyce Rupp.* One of my favorite books, this practical and well-written account offers candor and advice on how to walk this journey with a close friend. As an older trekker, the author shares honestly and meaningfully about her experiences and shares the importance of preparing and letting go of impractical expectations.

Two Million Step: Band-aids, Cocktails, and Finding Peace Along Spain's Camino de Santiago *by Patrick DeVaney.* As a middle-aged man going through a mid-life crisis, his is a very real rendition of meeting people and the challenges he faces while enjoying the wine, food, and friendship. His experience deepens as he walks, and he shares some of his unique realizations with the reader.

Strangers on The Camino, A Father, a Son, and a Holy Trail *by Sanjiva Wijesinha.* Described as "a tale about a middle-aged man who...took six weeks off a busy medical practice to spend this time with his adult son walking from one end of Spain to the other," he says his journey "turned out to be one of the best experiences of my life." His descriptions of moments spent with other pilgrims and his son are captivating and touching.

Buen Camino: What a Hike through Spain Taught Me about Investing and Life by *Gordon J. Bernhardt.* The author combines his experience along the Camino with lessons learned and wisdom achieved through years of advising and helping people. He intertwines his faith, experiences, and encounters into his own life-changing journey.

Pilgrim Strong, Rewriting my story on the Way of St. James by *Steve Watkins.* Forced by circumstances to reevaluate his own life, the author realizes he must come to terms with what his life means. The Camino offers him this opportunity, and he shares many side notes—things he learned along the way.

Grandma's on the Camino: Reflections on a 48-Day Walking Pilgrimage to Santiago by *Mary O'Hara Wyman.* Recommended by older pilgrims, this book describes Mary's journey at age 70. Through postcards and journal entries, she honestly shares her challenges, encounters, and insights about centering prayer.

Camino Sunrise, Walking With My Shadow by *Reginald Spittle.* Woven into the author's journey are memories of growing up with an emotionally distant father. I found these insights meaningful. He "comes out of the shadows" through trail-inspired moments and humorous incidents that connect the reader to his story.

Prancing in the Pyrénées, Sloshing Through Galicia, My Way Along the Camino Francés by *Suzanne Blazier.* The author is clear about her purpose for journeying the Camino: she likes to walk. Besides honest, no-nonsense descriptions of her experiences and how she dealt with sickness and feet issues, she has advice for anyone wanting to make the trek.

Senior Camino *by Donald Bowes.* A practical guide for anyone wanting to walk on the Camino, he includes sections to address mental, physical, and spiritual challenges. I especially appreciated what he says about being spiritually prepared and how he advises to "ask yourself the important questions before you go," like "What are my expectations?"

A Pilgrim's Guide to the Camino de Santiago, Camino Francés *by John Brierley.* A very thorough guide for any pilgrim walking on the traditional Camino, it includes details and information on how to make the trek. Some call it the *Camino Bible*. I recommend having a copy. You will find it helpful along the way, especially in the towns you pass through. He includes a great deal of information about albergues and places to stay along the way.

About the Author

At the Fervenza do Ezaro waterfall

Lele Beutel and her husband, Mike, enjoy traveling to new places. They have found that with each excursion come opportunities to make a difference in people's lives and have their own lives changed by others. Walking on the Camino de Santiago was one such adventure for Lele. She considers herself to be "secret agent" for God because of how He often leads her into unexpected situations where she's able to connect with others. Before retirement, she spent 25 years as a financial advisor and was able to encourage many people mentally, spiritually, and financially through her faith-based advice. Now, she and her husband spend time with their two dogs, Andey and Barney, with grandkids, and as volunteers at their church. They also share experiences with their life group members and the neighbors they meet while walking the dogs.

Other books she has written include: *What God Wants You to Know*, a 365-day devotional that reveals God's heart relating to passages from Genesis through Revelation; *From a Secret Place*, a daily devotional with questions and answers to and from God that came from 20 years of journaling; *The Reignbreaker*, a young adult fantasy; *Flora's Story*, about a young German refugee who miraculously escapes and survives the Nazi and Russian regimes of WWII Germany; and three books of poetry: *Lele's Lovesongs: Words of hope for the ones we love; Lele's Sighs: Reflections and Recollections;* and *Lele's Selah: Prayerful Poems that Inspire Hope.*

To reach her, you can find her on Facebook. Or email her at: *apedersen6@comcast.net.*

She would love to hear from you!

Read other books by Lele Beutel and follow on social media:

linktr.ee/authorlelebeutel